FEB 1976
RECEIVED
OHIO DOMINICAN
COLLEGE LIBRARY
COLUMBUS, OHIO
43219

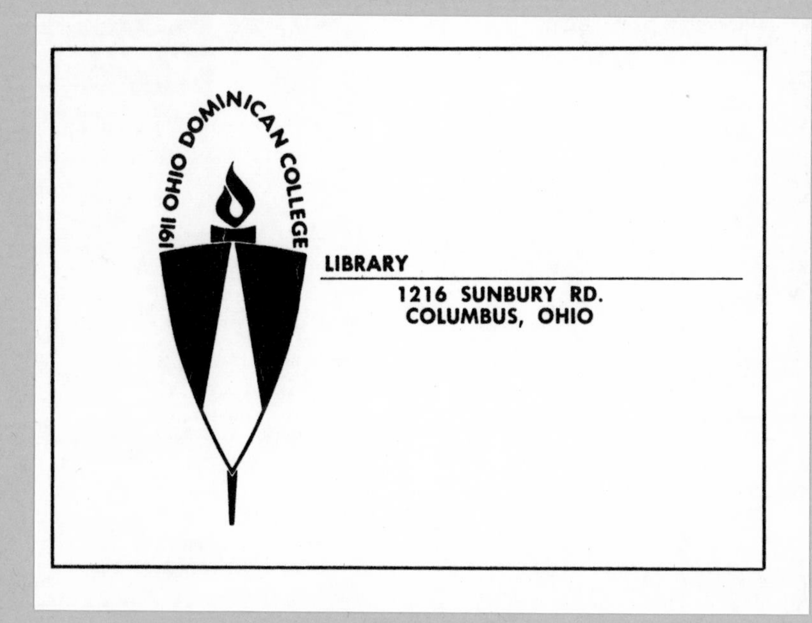
1911 OHIO DOMINICAN COLLEGE
LIBRARY
1216 SUNBURY RD.
COLUMBUS, OHIO

the Quixotic Vision of Sinclair Lewis

the Quixotic Vision of Sinclair Lewis

by Martin Light

Purdue University Press
West Lafayette, Indiana
1975

Library of Congress Card Catalog Number 74-82792
International Standard Book Number 0-911198-40-7
Printed in the United States of America

Contents

Preface

Seeing in Sinclair Lewis the perennial conflict between romance and realism (as others have done before me, particularly Mark Schorer and Sheldon Grebstein[1]), I shall here attempt to analyze it further as an expression of quixotism. Quixotism is an affliction that begins under the influence of readings in romantic literature and continues as a protagonist, thus inspired, ventures forth into a world he both finds and makes. Sinclair Lewis, as these pages shall show, was quixotic in his approach to life and recreated in his fiction the stories of significant quixotic heroes. This predilection led to a complex matrix of attitudes, for the inspiration of chivalry results on the one hand in foolish beliefs and behavior and on the other in kindness, generosity, sympathy, idealism. Furthermore, the impulse to reject romance leads to a vigorous sense of both comic exaggeration and realism, and Lewis was a humorist and a realist of considerable achievement.

In 1947 Professor Harry Levin declared that "Don Quixote's adventures in North America are still untraced"[2] (by adventures he meant influences upon literature), and even today the job has not been done. I intend to study here an author whose life and work seem to bear the characteristics of quixotism—a fondness for chivalric romance, from which an attitude toward life is taken, and a contradictory effort to examine, tame, expunge that attitude—a complicated matter.

Only occasionally has quixotism been discussed in American literature, chiefly by Joseph Harkey, Harry Levin, Ihab Hassan, and Theodore Gross.[3] My study of Sinclair Lewis may draw attention to the grasp that the quixotic archetype has had upon the imaginations of other American writers. For it appears not only in two of our earliest novels, *Modern Chivalry* and *Female Quixotism,* but also in the work of Irving, Melville, Mark Twain, Henry James, Sherwood Anderson, Hemingway, Fitzgerald, Wolfe, Faulkner, Salinger, and Bellow.

In *Life on the Mississippi* Mark Twain noted the return, in the nineteenth century, of the "medieval chivalry silliness" which *Don Quixote* had once swept away.[4] "That good work done by Cervantes" needed to be done again, and Mark Twain himself made the effort to do it. Sinclair Lewis, too, would attempt to clear the air, but he suffered from a significant disadvantage that made his attitude self-contradictory, namely that he loved romance, succumbing to it even as he fought it. And so it has been—and still is—with many people in America, especially as they respond to popular culture.

Popular culture is where Lewis chose to work as often as he strove for immortality in literary art.[5] His early life and early fiction, as my opening chapters show, reveal how deeply the elements of medievalism, chivalry, romance, and ideality lived within him. My central chapters report, where it is applicable (as it isn't quite, for instance, in *Elmer Gantry*), his best understanding and use of the quixotic imagination, from its full grasp upon Carol Kennicott to its release by Samuel Dodsworth. Lewis's later fiction includes a furious rejection of the quixote as writer (in Ora Weagle of *Work of Art*) even as it sketches out a number of weakly constructed idealists who show Lewis's continued affection for chivalric romance. By the end, in *The God-Seeker*, Lewis seems engaged in a desperate attempt (he had, after all, undergone some severe public and self-exploratory criticism) to justify his vision of America by creating the romantic ancestor of all his heroes, the pioneer Aaron Gadd. I conclude by discussing two fictional portraits of Lewis—by Hemingway and Wolfe—which seem to reflect, once again, the duality of his nature and his fiction, and the duality of critical responses to them. I hope, then, that this book will explain the work of Sinclair Lewis and bring him to our attention again, an attention which he surely deserves. I hope, also, that it will demonstrate the usefulness of looking at American literature from the point of view of quixotism.

The following is a list of first editions of books by Sinclair Lewis. In most cases they will be referred to in the text by obvious one- or two-word designations (such as *Wrenn, Hawk,* or *Arrowsmith*) with page numbers.

Hike and the Aeroplane. New York: Stokes, 1912 (written under the pseudonym of "Tom Graham").

Our Mr. Wrenn: The Romantic Adventures of a Gentle Man. New York: Harper, 1914.

The Trail of the Hawk: A Comedy of the Seriousness of Life. New York: Harper, 1915.

The Job: An American Novel. New York: Harper, 1917.
The Innocents: A Story for Lovers. New York: Harper, 1917.
Free Air. New York: Harcourt, Brace and Howe, 1919.
Main Street: The Story of Carol Kennicott. New York: Harcourt, Brace and Howe, 1920.
Babbitt. New York: Harcourt, Brace, 1922.
Arrowsmith. New York: Harcourt, Brace, 1925.
Mantrap. New York: Harcourt, Brace, 1926.
Elmer Gantry. New York: Harcourt, Brace, 1927.
The Man Who Knew Coolidge: Being the Soul of Lowell Schmaltz, Constructive and Nordic Citizen. New York: Harcourt, Brace, 1928.
Dodsworth. New York: Harcourt, Brace, 1929.
Ann Vickers. Garden City: Doubleday, Doran, 1933.
Work of Art. Garden City: Doubleday, Doran, 1934.
Selected Short Stories. Garden City: Doubleday, Doran, 1935.
It Can't Happen Here. Garden City: Doubleday, Doran, 1935.
The Prodigal Parents. Garden City: Doubleday, Doran, 1938.
Bethel Merriday. Garden City: Doubleday, Doran, 1940.
Gideon Planish. New York: Random House, 1943.
Cass Timberlane. New York: Random House, 1946.
Kingsblood Royal. New York: Random House, 1947.
The God-Seeker. New York: Random House, 1949.
World So Wide. New York: Random House, 1951.

Lewis's essays have been collected in *The Man from Main Street: A Sinclair Lewis Reader. Selected Essays and Other Writings, 1904–1950.* Eds. Harry E. Maule and Melville H. Cane. New York: Random House, 1953. When I quote from any essay printed therein, I will cite not only its original place of publication, but its location in the collection, the title of which I shall abbreviate as *MFMS.*

Some of Lewis's letters appear in *From Main Street to Stockholm: Letters of Sinclair Lewis, 1919–1930.* Selected and with an Introduction by Harrison Smith. New York: Harcourt, Brace, 1952. In footnotes, I shall refer to Lewis as "L," to Alfred Harcourt as "H," and to Donald Brace as "B." I will abbreviate the title of the book to *FMSTS.*

The biography of Lewis is Mark Schorer's admirable *Sinclair Lewis: An American Life.* New York: McGraw-Hill, 1961. I shall refer to it as *SL: Life.* A reminiscence by Lewis's first wife, Grace Hegger Lewis, is called *With Love from Gracie: Sinclair Lewis,*

1912–1925. New York: Harcourt, 1955. I shall refer to the book as *Gracie.*

I am indebted to Professor John T. Flanagan of the University of Illinois, who first read this book in a different form and gave me good criticism of it. I am also grateful to Professors Felix Stefanile and Harold Watts of Purdue University for discussing the subject matter with me and to Professor Richard Voorhees of Purdue for reading the manuscript in progress. I wish to thank the Purdue Research Foundation for support. I owe an additional debt to my wife Dorothy for her help along the way, and I wish to dedicate the book to her and to our children, Judith, Betsy, Kate, and Steven.

Acknowledgments

I would like to express my gratitude to the following for permission to quote from copyrighted works:

To *The Atlantic Monthly* for excerpts from "The Incorruptible Sinclair Lewis" by Perry Miller, copyright 1915, by the Atlantic Monthly Company, Boston, Mass. Reprinted with permission.

To *Newsweek* for excerpts from "Glorious Dirt" by Sinclair Lewis, copyright Newsweek, Inc. 1937. Reprinted by permission.

To the Cardavon Press, Inc., for quotations from the following: From "Foreword" to H. G. Wells: *The History of Mr. Polly,* copyright 1941 by The Readers Club, copyright 1969. From "Foreword" to J. B. Priestley: *Angel Pavement,* copyright 1942 by the Readers Club, copyright 1970. From "Introduction" to Sinclair Lewis: *Main Street,* copyright 1937 by the Limited Editions Club, copyright 1965. From "Introduction" to Ernest Hemingway: *For Whom the Bell Tolls,* copyright 1942 by the Limited Editions Club, copyright 1970. All used by permission of the Cardavon Press, Avon, Conn.

To Macmillan Publishing Company, Inc., for permission to quote from Warner Berthoff, *The Ferment of Realism: American Literature 1884–1919.* Copyright 1965 by the Free Press.

To the *Nation* for permission to quote from Sinclair Lewis, "Main Street's Been Paved," "Mr. Lorimer and Me," and "Minnesota, The Norse State."

To *Saturday Review/World* for permission to quote from Sinclair Lewis, "Literary Felonies" and William Rose Benét, "The Earlier Lewis."

To Hawthorn Books, Inc., for permission to quote from T. K. Whipple, *Spokesmen.*

To Charles Scribner's Sons for permission to quote from Ernest Hemingway, *Across the River and into the Trees.*

To Harper and Row, Publishers, Inc., for permission to quote from Thomas Wolfe, *You Can't Go Home Again.*

To the Viking Press, Inc., for quotations from *The Portable Carl Van Doren,* copyright 1936 by Carl Van Doren, renewed 1964 by Margaret Van Doren Bevans, Barbara Van Doren Klaw, and Anne Van Doren Ross. Reprinted by permission of the Viking Press, Inc.

To *New Letters* for excerpts from Allen Austin, "An Interview with Sinclair Lewis," reprinted by permission of *New Letters* (formerly *The University Review*), The University of Missouri–Kansas City.

To Harvard University Press for permission to quote from Willard Thorpe, *American Writing in the Twentieth Century,* copyright Harvard University Press, 1960.

To the Department of English, Harvard University, and to Harvard English Studies for excerpts from Harry Levin, "The Quixotic Principle" from *The Interpretation of Narrative: Theory and Practice,* edited by Morton W. Bloomfield.

To Random House, Inc., for permission to quote from *Gideon Planish, Cass Timberlane, Kingsblood Royal, The God-Seeker,* and *World So Wide* by Sinclair Lewis; also for permission to quote from "Self-Portrait (Berlin)" and "The Unpublished Introduction to *Babbitt,*" by Sinclair Lewis, from *The Man from Main Street: A Sinclair Lewis Reader,* edited by Harry E. Maule and Melville H. Cane, copyright Random House, Inc., 1953; and for permission to quote from *Homage to Theodore Dreiser* by Robert Penn Warren, copyright Random House, Inc., 1971.

To Alfred A. Knopf, Inc., for permission to quote from *Letters of H. L. Mencken,* edited by Guy J. Forgue, copyright Alfred A. Knopf, Inc., 1961.

To Ernst, Cane, Berner & Gitlin for permission to quote from "A Theory of Values," "Young Man Axelbrod," "Poems," "Breaking into Print," "Our Friend, H. G.," and "How I Wrote a Novel on Trains and beside the Kitchen Sink," all by Sinclair Lewis.

Excerpts from the following books by Sinclair Lewis are reprinted by permission of Harcourt Brace Jovanovich, Inc.: *Our Mr. Wrenn, The Trail of the Hawk, The Job, Free Air, Main Street, Babbitt, Arrowsmith, Mantrap, The Man Who Knew Coolidge, Elmer Gantry,* and *Dodsworth* copyright 1914, 1915, 1917, 1919, 1920, 1922, 1942, 1943, 1945, 1947, 1948, 1950, by Sinclair Lewis; copyright, 1926, 1927, 1928, 1929, by Harcourt Brace Jovanovich, Inc.; copyright, 1954, 1955, 1956, 1957, by Michael Lewis. Also excerpts from *From Main Street to Stockholm: Letters of Sinclair Lewis 1919–1930,* edited by Harrison Smith, quoted by permission of Harcourt Brace Jovanovich, publishers. And quotations from *With Love from Gracie* by Grace Hegger Lewis, by permission of Harcourt Brace Jovanovich, Publishers.

To the Viking Press for excerpts from *The Strange Necessity* by Rebecca West. Copyright 1928, renewed 1956 by Rebecca West. Reprinted by permission of the Viking Press, Inc.

To Mark Schorer for quotations from *Sinclair Lewis: An American Life,* copyright McGraw-Hill, 1961.

To *The American Scholar* and to Frederick Manfred for excerpts from "Sinclair Lewis: A Portrait" by Frederick Manfred, from *The American Scholar,* vol. 23, no. 2, Spring 1954. Copyright 1954 by the United Chapters of Phi Beta Kappa. By permission of the publishers and the author.

To *Arizona Quarterly,* where Chapter 6 appeared in a slightly different form as "The Quixotic Motifs of *Main Street,*" vol. 29 (Autumn 1973), copyright by *Arizona Quarterly.*

To *English Literature in Transition, Western Humanities Review,* and *New Letters* (formerly *University of Kansas City Review*) for copyrighted passages from articles of mine that appeared in those journals in somewhat different form.

To *The Yale LIT* for permission to quote from Sinclair Lewis, "The Fallacy of Elsewhere," copyright April 1906.

To *Cosmopolitan Magazine* for quotations from "I'm an Old Newspaperman Myself" by Sinclair Lewis, copyright 1947 by *Cosmopolitan Magazine.*

Chapter 1

Introduction

In an essay called "This Golden Half-Century, 1885–1935," Sinclair Lewis announced his metaphor for the age. Looking back over both the fifty years of his life and a simultaneous fifty years of his nation's literary and social history, he took his figure from nineteenth-century gentility's revival of interest in medievalism. His metaphor would express the quality of the era as he believed he had lived it and as he thought it had been lived by others.

The previous half-century had been an age, he wrote, "when there was romance everywhere, and life, instead of being a dusty routine, was exciting with hope and courage and adventure into utterly new lands."[1] In his time, Lewis went on, as when knighthood was in flower, "handsome young men in helmets rode the fastest steeds that ever had been known," and "maidens [danced] in silver and flowered silks." He directed the young to take up the challenges of their day fearlessly, even as he, toting his hopes of conquest, had ridden out into the world as a youth, with the exuberance of a knight. Arriving in New York City in 1903 (he wrote elsewhere), he was determined "to love the East . . . love it and dominate it," as it submitted to his "will to conquer."[2]

Throughout the years, he struggled to make this metaphor sustain him. If in 1935 he had been seeing realistically rather than through the spectacles of romance, he might have admitted the weaknesses of his metaphor. It could do little to portray a world that had suffered the agony of the immigrants' lot in the cities, had seen the revolt against village mind and ethos, had endured a great war, was deep in a depression, and was threatened by fascism and communism. As his own life and times should have shown him, to use this metaphor was to ignore at least half of experience, such experience as had been more accurately expressed in other metaphors such as jungle, prison, wasteland. For the moment Lewis disregarded all that and submitted to the enchanted vision of romantic medievalism. He was swept away, though he had the occasional capacity to look into the horrifying face of his illusions; as I shall attempt to show, the conflict of two visions was the impulse of his work, and his adherence to his metaphor rather than rejection of it was the source of his optimism and his misery.

Professor Lowry Nelson, Jr., points to "the trajectory of great fiction indebted to Cervantes from . . . Henry Fielding's *Tom Jones* to Stendhal's *The Red and the Black,* Gustave Flaubert's *Madame Bovary,* Herman Melville's *Moby Dick,* and Mark Twain's *Huckleberry Finn,* to mention only a few notable instances."[3] To these novels we may add Lewis's *Main Street* and *Arrowsmith*—and, ultimately, the whole body of his fiction, weak novels included. Important attempts to purge us of romanticism took place in the 1920s in the work of writers that Lewis knew well. Hemingway, for instance, had contrived a fiction in which a foolish idealist is sent packing: Robert Cohn, the avid reader of *The Purple Land* (an account of "splendid imaginary amorous adventures of a perfect English gentleman in an intensely romantic land," says Jake Barnes[4]), had been ridiculed, battered, defeated, and rejected in *The Sun Also Rises,* while Jake, the realist, who attempts to come to terms with his moment on earth, survives. In Fitzgerald's *The Great Gatsby,* Jay Gatsby, who had come onto the scene as the platonic creation of himself, was allowed a last romantic gesture, then was destroyed. Dreiser's *An American Tragedy* shows us Clyde Griffiths, who, driven by the inspiration of an Arabic evil genie, had committed murder and had been electrocuted in the testing and breaking of his illusions. But Sinclair Lewis's Arrowsmith, another character within this cluster of great novels published during that remarkable season of 1925 and 1926, was allowed to shape a survival; though defeated in his attempts to test his antitoxin under the most romantic, unmethodical conditions spun from his own fantasizing mind, he is allowed to withdraw to a shack in the woods, later, it is implied, to return to society, as he chooses, with his work accomplished.

Arrowsmith survives because he possesses the eternal optimism of the romanticist. The kind of romanticist who schools himself on sentimental novels, who sees himself as riding forth to conquer, and who finds a world that is more the projection of his illusions than the result of a sense of reality is called a quixote. The quixote has enduring hope, is blind to defeat, and walks down paths and into adventures of his own making.

A healthy imagination aids us in moving toward the future. At our most sane, we prepare for the life ahead of us with the help of a model of the life we wish to lead, and, if necessary, we adjust our imagined model as our confrontation with reality requires. The person with a quixotic imagination has a model also, but draws the patterns for it from romances and is seduced so completely by them that he cannot accommodate to reality but instead recreates it to suit his fancy. In the formulation invented by Cervantes, the quixote has been maddened by books. With his head full of idealism and illusion, the quixote goes forth to set injustices aright, to honor his lady, and to seek fame. Impelled by idealism to aid the weak and to combat injustice, he raises a challenge for the conventional community. The peculiarity of his challenge disconcerts the community and causes it to expose its own follies and corruptions. The quixote's madness can induce a maddened response in others, or at least unsettle them enough to reveal their hypocrisies. Thus the target of novels of quixotism can be both the hero and society. Satiric and ironic tension may arise from the conflict between the quixote and his community.

In explaining what he calls "the quixotic principle," Professor Harry Levin quotes Shaw and then Gide: it is "the tragicomic irony of the conflict between real life and the romantic imagination"; and it is "the rivalry between the real world and the representation that we make of it for ourselves."[5] But, says Levin, the quixotic principle is not a negative one "simply because it operates through [the quixote's] disillusionment. Rather, it is a register of development, an index of maturation. Its incidental mishaps can be looked back upon as milestones on the way to self-awareness."[6]

The quixote's problem is one of vision; his reading and his will to believe what he reads have left his vision distorted. He transforms what he sees into what his reading has led him to see, and indeed into what he now wishes to see. Windmills are perceived as giants. If he is told that the giants are nothing more than windmills (and if for a passing second he recognizes that they may possibly be so) he quickly declares that they only *appear* to be windmills, that they are enchanted giants nonetheless. Professor Levin writes, "In [*Don Quixote*] we behold a full-length portrait of a single-minded reader for whom reading is believing, and whose consequent distortions of reality help to sharpen our apprehension of it."[7]

Professor Richard Predmore lists three elements of the quixotic world: "literature, which is an all-pervasive presence and source of illusions; adventures, which arise from the clash between illusions and reality; and enchantment, which serves to defend illusions against inhospitable reality."[8] Applying a modification of this formula to Sinclair Lewis and the characters of his fiction, we will study them in terms of the way books create the imaginations of those who read them, in terms of the mission to redress wrongs in the community, and in terms of the need to romanticize or transform reality; in other words, we will study reading, adventure, and enchantment in Lewis and his characters.

Sinclair Lewis possessed the quixotic imagination, and many of his characters, who read, venture, and fancy, as he did, are inheritors of his vision. In him opposing emotions ran deep, yet surfaced quickly. Perhaps volatility goes hand-in-hand with the impulse to create a body of fiction that searches out and breaks stereotypes apart, pillories injustices, and exposes those beliefs we loosely call "myths" about the American way of living and the American character. In Lewis, the classic struggle between illusion and reality is particularly fierce—for Lewis's enemies were both the illusions he discovered in the world and the illusions his nature invented. He fought the illusions the world offered and struggled to understand the illusions his mind and emotions brought forth.

As a result, impudence, flamboyance, and audacity, at one extreme, and gloom, despair, and carelessness, at the other, characterize Lewis's books. Mark Schorer and others record Lewis's exuberant performances, deep angers, rantings, drunkenness, tasteless practical jokes, and contrition—the emotionalism of a distraught quixote who finds outlet in audacious gestures.[9]

Lewis stubbornly adhered to a few romantic ideas, personified in his books by yearners, rebels, and builders. His central characters are the pioneer, the doctor, the scientist, the businessman, and the feminist. The appeal of his best fiction lies in the opposition between his idealistic protagonists and an array of fools, charlatans, and scoundrels—evangelists, editorialists, pseudo-artists, cultists, and boosters.

Lewis was a crusader, a noisy presumptuous knight. With loud words and extravagant gestures he would thrust at listeners and readers. Picture Lewis as he appears in photographs—is there not some resemblance to illustrations of Don Quixote? Lewis is tall, lanky, of troubled eye, with a pock-marked face, ill-fitted by his clothes, often beside or inside a Ford that is his steed for riding forth to adventures; if occasionally angry, nonetheless pitying and kindly, and often very much alone, William Rose Benét, who was acquainted with young Lewis at Yale and in California, has left a vivid account of Lewis's early performances:

> There were . . . the almost endless monologues in which he suddenly took on a character part, and the fantastic imaginings that would be worked out in the most intricate detail, till one almost screamed for surcease from the spate of words. From intense hilarity the man would also, at times, turn as grave and didactic as a Baptist minister and proceed to lay down the moral law, according to his own highly individual ideas, with an almost snarling earnestness that seemed to bode hell-fire for the unbeliever.[10]

Throughout Lewis's life, he would make such flamboyant and egocentric gestures: in a restaurant, Lewis loudly imitates the boosterism of a babbitt; as he courts his first wife, he writes playful letters and poems in which he assumes the role of a jester and declares her to be a princess; he seeks the widest publicity for his letter turning down the Pulitzer award; to demonstrate to a church forum that God is not vengeful, he speaks against fundamentalist fear of Hell for fifteen minutes and invites God to strike him dead on the spot; on another occasion he rises to deliver a banquet address, proposes to Dorothy Thompson instead, and sits down. As an amusing example of Lewis's audacity, there is an episode from the apprentice years, when he was shaping a successful career as a writer. While working on *Main Street* (which he foresaw as a great success), he put to use the old skills learned during an earlier term as publicity writer in the Stokes publishing house. To advertise his most recent novel, *Free Air,* he suggested a plan characteristically egotistical and brash. He wrote to his publisher, Alfred Harcourt, "Here's an idea for an ad:

> Whenever you see the sign
> FREE AIR
> before a garage think of
> the one book that makes motoring romantic
> FREE AIR

Or something like that." And he comments, "We ought, somehow, to be able to take advantage of the publicity implied in all the tens of thousands of Free Air signs before garages and filling stations."[11] He would, one can believe, write his name on all the billboards of all the highways of the nation. He began one of his most important books, *Main Street,* with the announcement, "This is America," thus presuming to take the whole country as his subject. Lewis created his own state, Winnemac, in the Middle West, and his own cities, towns, and villages, with a mob of people to live in them.

For these reasons he is something beyond a realist. It may be closer to the truth to nominate him, as Constance Rourke proposed and Mark Schorer recently seconded, a "fabulist."[12] He had been labelled "journalist," "photographer," "realist," and "satirist." Some of these labels were offered, I think, to suggest that he was a literalist and that he lacked "imagination." However, he counterbalanced his literalness not only with imagination but with "fancy." *Fancy* is a term he often used himself (both when speaking in his own voice and when speaking through the voices of his characters). Still innocent and still assembling an inner world which they hope they will find in the outer one, his young, idealistic, and adventuring characters fancy; they fancy the long-ago, the far-away, and the exotic. Nevertheless, they, and others of his figures whom the plot puts in their path, "observe"—that is, they examine and document reality. But his fancy is the symptom of his quixotism. He is the quixote who projects his inner world upon the external experience, while reality hammers at him for attention. Fancy drew him as much as observation did. Though he delighted in fancy, he was often suspicious of it; it is a trivial, whimsical attribute, but he thought it could be converted to good use.

Many of Lewis's characters are full of fancy, yet his heroes and heroines will waken to an awareness of reality. Lewis himself started out as a young vagabond, and, like a knight seeking the Grail, he quite deliberately built his career, advertised himself, and sought the literary prizes. He attained the goal of his quest when he stepped to the dais in Stockholm, where he was cited and praised for his social satire, his creation of original characters, and his wit and humor.[13] From the podium, as the first American to win the Nobel Prize for literature, he could address not merely the Nobel Prize Committee, but his country and the world.

Living in a time when the form and function of the novel were being redefined, Lewis commented upon his own fiction in contradictory and ambivalent ways. He was aware of a conflict between his impulse toward romance and his impulse toward realism. Furthermore, like the clown who wishes to play Hamlet, he self-consciously rededicated himself, at frequent intervals throughout his career, to turn from the comic novel to the novel of heroic proportions and tragic consequences. In several essays and letters he tried to explain himself and his work. He seemed to be seeking metaphors beyond knight or jester. As early as 1920, just after the publication of *Main Street*, his first important book (though his seventh in print, if we include a potboiler for teenagers), he encountered, for example, Carl Van Doren's aspersions about "propaganda" in his novels and responded with a pledge to keep his next book as far as possible from that defect; he hoped, he wrote to Van Doren, to enable his projected portrait of the Tired Business Man to "live." A year later, again writing to Van Doren, he protested that a careful reading of *Our Mr. Wrenn, The Trail of the Hawk*, and especially *The Job* would reveal that he was not simply a writer of clever "vaudeville" (as Van Doren had called him) but a "serious workman" capable of tenderness, honest realism, sobriety, and genuine love for (not merely abuse of) his fictional creations.[14] In addition, letters to his publisher indicate that during the writing of *Babbitt*, Lewis was struggling with the problems of characterization in terms of *type* and *individual*, intending that Babbitt be something of the first, yet feeling that he also must be much of the second if the novel were to have the depth Lewis wanted it to have. Again, after the publication of *Babbitt*, Lewis asserted that his intimations for the next novel were "non-satiric."[15] That book was to be a serious portrait of a saintly labor leader patterned after Eugene Debs. When, however, he abandoned the labor project, it was in part because he had found another affirmative hero, far more congenial to his fancy, in the physician-scientist Martin Arrowsmith.

From this point onward, Lewis defined himself both as an experimental diagnostician and as a preacher, but always as a worker or builder. To moderate whatever image of himself the public, aided by antagonistic critics, may have formed, he would say that he merely scoffed at or dissected his subject, that he was actually kindly, cheerful, and sentimental, in love with America. Upon rereading his short stories in order to publish a selection of them, he discovered that he was not simply a satirist, but at heart a "romantic medievalist."[16] If he displayed a hatred, it was hatred of hypocrisy and of bunk, not of people.[17] "I'm not a cynic," he said. "I'm an old evangelist—a moral evangelist preaching to my people. . . . Really I should have been a preacher. . . . either a preacher or a doctor."[18] "I'm different from Mencken. I think he despises the American people. Actually I'm scolding them like children."[19]

He kept to his craft. He testified that he composed a novel while riding the train to and from his advertising job and that he labored like a ditch-digger. Of the hard work of producing a novel, Lewis said, "It has been a good job and, even when it has been rather sweaty and nerve-jangling, I have enjoyed it more than I would have enjoyed anything except pure research in a laboratory."[20] He said, "I would give a lot if . . . I could go to work in a biological laboratory, or possess an inn of my own to fuss over . . . or be able to build a chicken house."[21]

Lewis once wrote a mock obituary of himself, indicating how he wished to be remembered. He made much of the fact that though born a Midwesterner he possessed New England ancestry and had recently owned a farm in Vermont. He pictured himself, then, as the "Last Surviving Connecticut Yankee," who, when sought out by a visiting professor of literature, was to be discovered "at a local garage, playing pinochle with the village constable-undertaker." At his death, so Lewis predicted, Carl Van Doren would be heard to observe: "This was a good workman and a good friend, who could still laugh in days when the world had almost worried itself out of the power of laughter."[22] It appears, then, that if he defined himself both as a skeptical yet congenial satirist and as a romantic, it was because he wanted it known that he could be at once disgusted with people and fond of them. Not "arty" nor a wastrel, he was a craftsman and a worker. While still at college the young and idealistic Lewis had written of the "spark" that was in every man—"that spark which makes him wonderful."[23] Midway in his career, in defense of himself against the label of cold-hearted satirist, Lewis had paused to call the roll of those of his characters to whom he had given what he believed to be admirable attributes and emotions: Max Gottlieb, for his learning, integrity, accuracy, and achievement; Leora Tozer, as an embodiment of love and loyalty; Babbitt, possessor of deep and authentic affection for his son and for his friend Paul; Carl Ericson and Frank Shallard, men of courage; and Will Kennicott, a skillful and resolute physician.[24]

But the necessity to call attention to the positive aspects of his characters only reminds us of his more obvious abiding interest in the peculiar ones—the grotesque, the inconsistent, and the hypocritical ones—that abound in his work. As his heroes venture forth, subjects for criticism meet their eyes everywhere. When Lewis felt called upon to make some declarations about his idea of the novel, he said that he saw it as the medium by which he could expose hypocrisy; he hated

> politicians who lie and bully and steal under cover of windy and banal eloquence, and doctors who unnecessarily and most lucratively convince their patients that they are ill; merchants who misrepresent their wares, and manufacturers who pose as philanthropists while underpaying their workmen; professors who in wartime try to prove that the enemy are all fiends, and novelists who are afraid to say what seems to them the truth.[25]

In fact, attacking hypocrites was the principal task of his life and work, as the Nobel speech testifies.

Almost twenty years after Benét had seen young Lewis performing his monologues, we hear Lewis himself suggesting the uses he had learned to put his mimicry to. "This Lewis," he fondly imagined his auditors saying after he had entertained them with a babbitt-like monologue, "is giving us the very soul of a character, and through him of a civilization."[26] It is no modest assumption to believe that one has created characters that will represent a civilization—the America of 1920 to 1945. In ensuing chapters we will measure out the extent to which he succeeded in achieving his goal.

Here let me call one of Lewis's characters forward to exemplify the way quixotism functions in his work. It is the protagonist of *Main Street*, young Carol Milford (soon to be Carol Kennicott), who had fed her imagination on "village-improvement" (pictures of "greens and garden-walls in France"), who had, at the banks of the Mississippi, "listened to its fables about the wide land of yellow waters and bleached buffalo bones to the West," and who had thought of "Southern levees and singing darkies" and palm trees and river steamers and Dakota chiefs; she stands on the High Bridge across the Mississippi and sees Yang-tse villages below. She fancies turning "a prairie town into Georgian houses and Japanese bungalows." Her conversation, we are told, is some modern equivalent of that of Elaine and Sir Launcelot. Her mind is filled by images of "elsewhere." Yet her plan is to create a hometown that will fulfill her vision. She articulates her ambitions by saying, "I'll get my hands on one of these prairie towns and make it beautiful." Soon this quixotic girl meets that other American prototype, the practical man. Doctor Kennicott, courting Carol in St. Paul, attempts to persuade her to come to Gopher Prairie with him by showing her a dozen snapshots of the town. The pictures are "streaky." But her fanciful vision overcomes the reality of the photographs. At first she can see only "trees, shrubbery, a porch indistinct in leafy shadows." But she creates what she wants to see and exclaims over the lakes, bluffs, ducks, and fishermen, and then a "clumsy log cabin chinked with mud, . . . a sagging woman . . . a baby bedraggled." Moved by his love, Kennicott deceives her: "Just look at that baby's eyes, look how he's begging—." She answers in self-delusion: "Oh, it would be sweet to help him—." What follows is four hundred pages of lessons in how to see and what to believe, lessons regrettably never firmly learned. Lewis's books are attempts at correct viewing. The whole life's work is the study of illusions and realities. Lewis, having begun with a vacuous and misleading set of illusions, makes us witness, down through the years, the same ritual encounter between illusion and reality. He repeatedly brings his illusions before us and then destroys them. And he cries out both for what is lost and against the agents of betrayal. Fortunately, he can also surround the ritual in comedy, and the comedy pleases us.

Lewis's flaws of style and some of his puerile notions will remain a problem for every reader. But perhaps one way to approach his novels is this: He was a great talker. He began as an admirer of a bad "literary" language, but he learned the uses of common speech. He employed the comic potential of the vernacular to expose the boosters and hypocrites he saw in American life. As T. K. Whipple so well put it, he stalked the enemy like a Red Indian.[27] He was a demon of anger toward waste and cruelty. Yet he was sympathetic and could give in to a whimsical imagination, which sought solace in places governed by a romanticized chivalric code. He began his career as a journalist and publicist, and perhaps always thought in terms of giant typography, headlines, billboards. There is amplitude in his best books, and if he is read for size—for his large quixotic vision—then his faults, in his best books at least, accordingly diminish. Before examining his novels closely, however, we will look at Lewis himself through his reading and literary involvements, through his adventures, and through his fantasies.

Chapter 2

Reading

Sinclair Lewis once said of himself that he was "afflicted with Wanderlust," which he called "one of the most devouring of diseases."[1] It is the disease of the quixote and is contracted by reading. Lewis was a great reader and wanderer. He was born Harry Sinclair Lewis in the frontier Minnesota village of Sauk Centre on February 7, 1885. At thirteen he tried to run away from home to join the army fighting the Spanish-American War. During all his life thereafter, he moved about this country and the world in a manner amazing to comprehend. Leaving Sauk Centre for pre-university training at Oberlin College, he then began adventures which included a journey to Yale, where he earned a degree, two cattleboat visits to England, a summer vacation in Minnesota, an unsuccessful search for a job in Panama, a short term as a newsman in Iowa, more than a year's stay in Carmel and San Francisco, and a term in Washington, D.C., as junior editor of a magazine for the deaf—all this before he entered New York City in 1910 at the age of twenty-five.

Lewis stayed in New York for five years. In 1912 he met a young woman on an elevator in a New York office building. She was Grace Livingstone Hegger, the princess of a quixote's dreams, a new feminist, and a glorious playfellow. He courted her for almost two years, and they were married on April 15, 1914. They set up housekeeping, but soon he was on the move again. His own summary of his travels during the years 1915 to 1930 tells us that he visited forty states of the Union, plus Canada, Mexico, England, Scotland, France, Italy, Sweden, Germany, Austria, Czechoslovakia, Yugoslavia, Greece, Switzerland, Spain, the West Indies, Venezuela, Colombia, Poland, and Russia.[2] Neither a home nor the birth of his son Wells Lewis could keep him domesticated. His eye began to wander to various women. In the twenties he and Grace were apart much of the time. Lewis wanted to maintain a convenient relationship which would allow him freedom to roam; at the same time his letters ask for a return to an atmosphere in which he and his wife could continue as Aucussin and Nicolette or troubadour and princess. By 1927, however, they had met the persons they were to marry next. Lewis had fallen in love, again at first sight, with the journalist Dorothy Thompson, and in flamboyant style not only at once asked her to marry him, but continued to do so on every occasion. Grace Lewis obtained a divorce in 1927, and Sinclair Lewis and Dorothy Thompson were married soon after.

Lewis and his bride travelled widely in Europe, then settled at Pomfret, Vermont. But again neither home nor the birth of Michael Lewis could restrain him from travelling. Dorothy Thompson's career was an increasing source of irritation to him. Their marriage ended in divorce in 1941. Lewis's relationship with Marcella Powers provided him with some companionship for several years. His first son was killed in World War II.

For short periods Lewis established homes in Duluth, Minnesota, and in Williamstown, Massachusetts. His frenetic movement always ended in dissatisfaction. He thought he needed roots. "Why," he records a friend's having asked him in 1942, "do I return for considerable stay in Minnesota? I try to answer: in New York, because of distance from Provinces, one does not return to native heath often . . . and one loses contact with roots."[3] Therefore, his diary entry for the next day reveals him at the graves of his paternal grandfather and grandmother. But near the end of his life, even after suffering pneumonia and a heart attack, he took to the road again. He was in Italy during the final year, and having recovered some strength, he restlessly began another tour of France and Switzerland. There were two more attacks in Zurich. He returned to Rome, where he died several months later, on January 10, 1951. His ashes were buried in Sauk Centre; his grave lies between the graves of his father and mother.

Wandering gets its impulse from books, and books have the further effect of inspiring fancy. To trace the literary influences on the novels of Sinclair Lewis, we can start when he was about fifteen, the age at which he began to think of himself as a writer. He was equipped with energy, determination, and genius. But his impulses were diffuse, and for a long time (perhaps until he discovered how to use the fictions of H. G. Wells as models in the completion of his first novel in 1914) Lewis followed many examples, traditions, and whims in various directions. The literary situation from about 1900 to 1920 (Lewis's apprentice years) supplied him with a tradition of great antecedent writers of the nineteenth century and some provocative innovators in the twentieth, but it also provided temptations into foolish and wasteful byways. Down all of these byways, it would seem, the quixotic young Lewis was eager to travel. Having chosen his metaphor from Scott, Tennyson, and the tales of King Arthur, he was a knight, riding out to conquer the publishing world and win princess and prizes. Over the years he gradually separated himself from some of the most absurd notions of his time and from some of its most mistaken modes of literary expression. He learned to exploit that separation in satire, putting himself forward then as a court jester, who, motivated either by rebuff or by disillusionment, exploited his great talent for mimicry; sometimes when deflated from his high expectations, he saw himself as a fool.

The chief business of the era from 1880 to 1919 was, as Warner Berthoff points out, the establishment of realism "as the dominant standard of value"—that is to say, the establishment of a method of reproducing life as lived and language as spoken.[4] To move forward, realism braced itself against and pushed off from nineteenth-century romanticism, which had brought forth giant figures, such as Emerson, Whitman, and Melville, who, by the nineties, were aged or recently dead. At the same time, perhaps because at the turn of the century the pathways were not crowded by such giants (except for Mark Twain, Henry James being abroad), opposition arose among sentimentalists, who wrote for women's magazines or extolled the villages in collections of essays or penned historical novels and verse on medieval subjects. By these means, in an outpouring of popular novels, the romantic mind countered upstart realism. For many of these writers, "fancy" was more highly valued than "observation"; "fancy" had a quality more airy than "imagination," a quality more capricious and beauteous. Accounts of real life, especially as it was being lived on midwestern farms and in ghettos, threatened established organizations. Berthoff says, "It is difficult now to imagine the hostility aroused in the high-minded by only a small degree of common candor in books."[5] The function of literature, the high-minded believed, was to uplift the spirit and to encourage optimism. Robert Penn Warren says, "The Romantic Movement had discovered—or created—the Middle Ages, and had prepared for them their sacred place in nineteenth-century thought and art. Tennyson's *Idylls of the*

King ranked in the esteem of the pious only a little lower than the New Testament, and James Russell Lowell's 'The Vision of Sir Launfal' was a close contender for the popularity prize with the Book of Common Prayer. . . ."[6]

The village itself was an important battleground for writers. Some sentimentalized and romanticized it; there lay warmth and kindliness. Meredith Nicholson called the Midwest "the Valley of Democracy," and praised folksiness. Booth Tarkington's hero in *The Gentleman from Indiana* (1900) says that he has had a feeling that the people of the Midwest have more sense and are kinder than people of the East. "The mood in the novels of the day is buoyant and optimistic," Willard Thorpe notes.[7] In popular books like *Mrs. Wiggs of the Cabbage Patch, The Little Shepherd of Kingdom Come, Rebecca of Sunnybrook Farm,* and *The Girl of the Limberlost,* the general message was that all is well. Yet this literary activity was, as Thorpe says, "at variance with the social changes of the Progressive Era, a period marked by the growth of the power of labor, the reform of municipal politics, the regulation of the giant trusts, and the demand for an end to the pillaging of our national resources."[8] As if to encourage further escape from reality, a series of novels appeared that took the reader into the past and the far-away; for example, *When Knighthood Was in Flower, Richard Carvell, Janice Meredith,* and *The Call of the Wild.* At the same time, the quality of contemporary life—especially life in the villages—was being closely observed by such writers as Howe, Eggleston, Frederic, Mark Twain, and Garland. Lewis was aware of some of this rebellious literature as early as 1905 and had read most of it by 1920, by which time he also knew the work of Dreiser, Anderson, and Masters, and would be identified with the movement which came to be called "the revolt from the village."

But Lewis as a young man was still ripe for the attractions of the romantic vision. He had been reading *Sentimental Tommy, Rupert of Hentzau, Under the Dog Star, The Christian, Nicholas Nickelby, Kim,* and *Kenilworth;* then more Scott—*The Talisman* and *The Antiquary*—and more Dickens—*Little Dorrit* and *Martin Chuzzlewit*—and *Adam Bede, The Hound of the Baskervilles, Pilgrim's Progress,* Washington Irving, and *Idylls of the King.* Soon he added "The Vision of Sir Launfal" (a favorite), more Kipling, and Browning, Keats, Swinburne, then Richard LeGallienne, Maeterlinck, Shaw, and H. G. Wells. There could be additional titles and writers on the booklist, but the essential observation to make is that here were an impressive number of romantics, sentimentalists, adventurers, and fantasists to nourish the young quixote.

The verse of the moment was the work of the genteel writers, those devoted to Ideality. The proper function of literature, they believed, was to elevate the spirit. Ideality, says Willard Thorpe, was "the world of dreams in which the poet's spirit wanders, unfettered from the False and free to seek the (ideally) True."[9] Ideality was fostered by a group of writers, editors, and professors, like Stedman, Aldrich, Stoddard, Taylor, Wendell, and Van Dyke. The work that some of these men produced is an embarrassment to read, but because Lewis imitated it, I should like to suggest its flavor. There was an infatuation with the far-away (India or Arabia, for example) expressed in what was intended as appropriately exotic and elevating language, as in Thomas Bailey Aldrich's "An Arab Welcome":

> Because thou com'st, a weary guest,
> Unto my tent, I bid thee rest.
> This cruse of oil, this skin of wine,
> The tamarinds and dates are thine;
> And while thou eatest, Medjid, there,
>   Shall bathe the heated nostrils of thy mare.
> Illah il' Allah! . . .[10]

Other titles in Aldrich's book of collected poems are "A Turkish Legend," "Two Songs from the Persian," "The Sultana," and (in the medieval mode) "Friar Jerome's Beautiful Book." A volume of poems by Bliss Carman and Richard Hovey, called *Songs from Vagabondia,* begins

> Off with the fetters
> That chafe and restrain!
> Off with the chain!
> Here Art and Letters
> Music and wine,
> And Myrtle and Wanda,
> The winsome witches,
> Blithely combine.
> . . .
> Here are the Indies,
> Here we are free—

Free as the wind is,
Free as the sea,
Free!
Houp-la![11]

Thus, as Aldrich's "Proem" says, "We weave our fancies, so and so."

In an essay for the "Editor's Table" of the *Yale Literary Magazine* (December 1906), Lewis called Stedman's "Aucassin and Nicolette" "as fine a lyric as we Americans have had." Its diction includes "ma belle," "ma très-douce mie," "droning priests," "barefoot monks and friars," "minstrels," "lusty knights," "men of valor," "beauteous ladies," "merry brides," "cithern strings," and "Pardie!" The bouncing melody, as well as the diction, suggests Stedman's standard of art and beauty.

Warner Berthoff lists some of the literary and social movements of the era—the experiments, if you wish, or the foolish indulgences that avoided the main business of the time:

> There was the cult of Bohemianism, and the accessory cults of the far away or long ago, the esoteric, the theosophic and occulto-cabalistic, all features of the '90s in particular [but obviously continuing to 1910 and beyond]. There was the cult of aestheticism—"art for art's sake" being art specifically not for the competition of the popular market. . . . There was, in another direction, the cult of "vagabondia," popularized in the poems of Richard Hovey and the Canadian Bliss Carman and exploited by Jack London, and the even heartier cult of the "strenuous life," endorsed between 1901 and 1909 by the White House itself.[12]

These cults had some appeal for the young, especially for provincial youths. In his short reminiscence called *Intellectual Vagabondage*, Floyd Dell has left an account of his own wanderings down various byways of the time.[13] Dell was only two years younger than Lewis, and there is a significant resemblance between the intellectual vagabondages of the two writers. There was a similar pattern in the books that were read and the ideas discussed. That generation had a love affair with the Middle Ages, Dell says. The medieval world was the center of orbit for Tennyson, Browning, Morris, and Swinburne. Fitzgerald's *Omar* turned imaginations eastward; Kipling inspired their interest in travel. Women came to see men as inefficient fools. For their part, the younger men were willing to take the new woman as an equal and companion—but (significantly) as a companion of their play rather than of their work; they sought a "glorious playfellow" (and few sought her more hopefully than

Lewis—or wrote about her more often until about 1919). Love would thrive outside marriage. Work itself would undergo reform, as capitalism gave way to socialism. Life would be an adventure—and that word *adventure,* too, moved to the forefront of talk and writing. Yet, finally, Dell finds that most of these ideas—medievalism, vagabondage, feminism, play, bohemianism, adventure, socialism, art for art's sake—failed to prepare the advancing generation for responsibility. To the rescue, he says, came H. G. Wells, who satirized cranks and fools, and whose fictional young men would assist in the disintegration of society and then in its reconstitution.

Lewis eagerly pursued socialism, vagabondage, and medievalism until he, like Dell, became disenchanted. He maintained, however, a simultaneous interest in realism, which had its expression in his diary. There he set down his observations; for example, he recorded what he saw during two brief voyages to England and one to Panama. He listed facts in statistical detail—the day's routine, the food and the sleeping situation, the yearnings of the men on ship, their slang, and some character sketches.[14] He found voice for realism in several pieces he wrote for Yale's literary journals. If we look at some of his Yale writing, we can see the crosscurrents of romance and realism that swept him—to put it simply, the influence of Scott and Stedman and the influence of Dickens and Garland.

To make too much of a writer's apprentice work may be unfair to him; he should have the privilege of concealing what he wishes to. But in Lewis's case, the Yale writing is too illuminating to pass without attention; it sets before us the contrasting subjects and modes he used. If it were true that Lewis matured quickly away from the romantic excesses we see here, they would be of little significance. But for a dozen years Lewis continued to write in the romantic mode, though he wrote some realistic tales as well. The romantic poetry continued until he was about thirty years of age, and the realism only gradually supplanted it. It can be argued that the conflict continued even in his best years, when he was struggling with both romance and realism, and when romantic attitudes, characterizations, and images persisted that had become ingrained in his mind quite early (that in fact he had chosen to drill into his way of thinking by constant practice). To a considerable extent he was representative, during the years 1900 to 1920, of a struggle within American literature, which was both nostalgic and rebellious, conservative and reformist.

Lewis's contribution to the *Yale Courant* in March 1906 was "Saint Hubert"; the poem went, in part, like this:

> Could St. Anselm's logic
> Make wine the less ruddy?
> St. George was too fiery,
> His dragon too bloody.
>
> Sing ho! for St. Hubert,
> The patron for me.
> When hunting horns wind
> Over heather and lea.

Fragments of other poems follow:

> Along the streets of rich Bagdad,
> In gold-embroidered silks yclad,
> With glittering cavalcade doth ride
> The caliph Haroun Alraschide. . . .
> ("When Viziers Speak")
>
> Come! A jolly story,
> Not of toil and glory,
> Not of killing, gory;
> But of a daisy-dale. . . .
> ("A Summer's Tale")
>
> The May time, the gay time,
> The merry, the faerie, the fay time.
> Alone do I ride,
> A lass at my side;
> By night and by moonlight, or day time. . . .
> ("A May Time Carol")

Occasionally some of this romanticizing appeared in his prose, dressed still in its special vocabulary; here is the opening of a short story: "Once upon a time,—as the nursery faerie tales begin,—there lived a princess yclept Selon, who was very learned, and passing fair withal. Gogwounds! How she captivated the king's sons thereabouts!"[15] His tone gently mocks these fancies, but he is captivated by them also.

Such is the poetry and prose Sinclair Lewis often wrote before college, in college, and for several years after college—in fact, during a fifteen-year period. His fancy dwelt upon the medieval princess, and the passage that follows here introduces a role which Lewis himself played in real life: ". . . At her feet crouches the little court fool, looking up into her deep eyes of green and hoping for a smile at least." As Larzer Ziff has said about the midwestern imagination in general, ". . . when the farm boy found himself driven to literary expression, then what came nimbly from his pen was, most frequently, tales of knights in the days of yore or of pioneer lasses braving the wilds. . . ."[16]

But another current of literature also moved within Lewis. In April 1906 the *Yale Monthly Magazine* printed his short story called "A Theory of Values." In style, tone, and theme, it is quite different from what we have already seen from Lewis's pen. In "A Theory of Values" Lewis tried his hand at realism and expressed himself not in medievalisms but in the vernacular. It is a story of aspiration, of hard work, and of disappointment. It opens with a letter from Karl Nelson to James Bradford, a student at the University of Minnesota. Karl thanks Jim for having shown him the metropolitan world of Minneapolis. Karl expresses his yearnings: "I want to do something in and for the world; not rot away in this dull, little town, and die unheard of. Here there is nothing to do; and I want to be doing—doing—doing." Karl glances at his mother who, "like many of the prisoners of the farm cook-stove, . . . had toiled till she was as shapeless as a bag of potatoes." Because there is a mortgage to pay, Karl goes to work in a store, where, "above the shelves of fly-specked canned goods, rose a vision of the Minneapolis he had seen from the court-house tower." But the vision fades and "the reality of the rows of cans and boxes remained."

The seasons pass and Karl's need for a job prevents his getting to the university. Finally, he admits to himself that he has to give up hope of college. One day he reads in the paper about the students' pranks. " 'What chumps they are,' laughed Karl. 'They are fooling around, instead of saving money, like me. . . .' " To his mother he says, " 'Let's be good and go to bed like dad has.' . . . And as he drowsily clumped up the narrow stairs, thinking of the morrow's work, he hummed 'Mandy.' " The story contains several pre-visions of Lewis's staple characterations of the twenties: the yearner, the worker or doer, and the plain, tired man clumping up to bed.

Hamlin Garland's perception of the Middle West probably influenced "A Theory of Values." One can see reflections of Garland's entrapped farmer and of the woman broken by her chores. Just before Lewis returned from Yale to spend the summer of 1905 in Sauk Centre, he read Garland, among other authors. Twenty-five years later he paid tribute to the powerful effect that *Main-Travelled Roads* and *Rose of Dutcher's Coolly* had upon him. Reading these books in just such an environment as Garland described, Lewis found them "vastly exciting." Balzac and Dickens had led him to understand that it was possible to be realistic in descriptions of French and English common people. But it had never occurred to him "that one might without indecency write of the people of Sauk Centre, Minnesota, as one felt about them." The fictional tradition of his times was that all inhabitants of midwestern villages were noble and happy. But in Garland's work, he discovered "that there was one man who believed that Midwestern peasants were sometimes bewildered and hungry and vile—and heroic." Given that vision, he was "released"; he could "write of life as living life."[17] Let us remember, however, that Lewis's account of this release came a quarter century after the fact; Garland surely opened one path for the creative energies of young Lewis, but in actuality Lewis's mind was still absorbed by the medieval vision. Innumerable poems and stories took that inspiration instead.

He was not entirely unaware that escape into far-away places was an imprudent temptation. The popular fiction of the day—books by Richard Harding Davis, Kipling, LeGallienne, Major—appealed to him, yet worried him. To call himself back from romance, he composed a piece for the April 1906 *Literary Magazine* about "the fallacy of elsewhere." He points to Zola-like subjects near at hand rather than in the distance. He explains that a Yale student can learn a great deal about life if, instead of yearning for distant shores, he will just observe what is around him; he will see slums in New Haven and can stroll on Oak Street on the Jewish Sabbath or at three in the morning when rats frisk on the sidewalks. He can visit a "delightful dive on Fair Street," or hear the "tale of the murder of a policeman in a terrible battle in New Haven's worst alley." He will find "the folk of the night." Lewis lists many other places: the house where Jonathan Edwards courted a woman; the one the ghost of Samuel Morse haunts; the cemetery where Eli Whitney, Noah Webster, and Harriet Beecher Stowe's father are buried. He concludes: "When the Wanderlust sends you in fancy to Paris or India, take a still longer voyage in that terra incognita, New Haven!"

In another essay for the magazine, in June 1906, he attempts to prick the bubble, as he calls it, of the "overestimated men," and he defends the "unknown undergraduates"—like himself, one suspects. He speaks of a young man from the farm, with no heredity and no friends, who has struggled alone and won every battle. He points out that "there are men who have yet to find themselves," and who will succeed later in life; he asks patience for them.[18] Such a man he has already put into fiction; it is Karl. And such he will put into fiction many times again, once especially in a story of Yale called "Young Man Axelbrod."

Much, then, attracted him in the eager days of his youth; and gradually much came to repel him. He indulged himself in fancy, dreaming of knights riding forth, of pioneers, of Indians, of princesses, of vagabond adventures in far-off places. He responded also to the realistic treatment of life and language in Balzac, Garland, and Dreiser—to the pictures of kitchens and fields and hard-working men and women, and of lives stunted and ambitions thwarted.

What will interest us, I think, is to see the elements of fancy and observation contending within Lewis, as he works his way from acceptance of not just the charm but the truth of fancy, through an extended inner argument (which he projects outward into characterizations), toward an acknowledgment of the merits of realism. For support he will rely upon the useful diary. Then he replaces the diary with his elaborate notebooks. In addition, he discovers the uses of satire. Like Dell and many other writers, he finds the models of satire not only in Dickens (whom he much admired) but, more accessibly, in H. G. Wells.

Of the authors whose work Sinclair Lewis read in his youth, Dickens had a great influence upon him. He called Dickens his idol. Lewis recalled that it seemed perfectly natural and inevitable for a young writer of about 1910 (Lewis was then in his mid-twenties) to use Dickens as a model by which to make social comedy out of America—so reported Professor Perry Miller, who talked with Lewis during an Atlantic crossing in 1949.[19] Lewis elsewhere paid highest tribute to Dickens. What he admired was not simply the social commentary and the reforming impulse, but Dickens's *evocation* of the social milieu—the vast London of his day—and Dickens's creation of a great number of memorable characters. "Only those of the young generation who have created one-hundredth of the characters born of Dickens," Lewis wrote, "have a right to sneer at him."[20]

We should note that Pickwick, primary among Dickens's characters, is a quixote.

Between Dickens and H. G. Wells, Lewis saw "a link that is the clearer the more one thinks of it."[21] His praise for Wells was always in the superlative. In "The Passing of Capitalism," an essay published in *Bookman* in November 1914, Lewis said that Wells might justly be called "the greatest living novelist," and he appeared never to change that belief. Some twenty-seven years later he could say, "It seems probable to me that just now, in 1941, there is no *greater* novelist living than Mr. H. G. Wells. On the mountainous slopes of Thomas Mann, there are too many fogs of magic for the bulk of him to overshine the quick, plump, gaily trotting human figure of Wells."[22] Wells, Lewis said, excited the young minds of 1910 to 1930 more than did even Shaw or the Huxleys or any writer of this century (notice that in Lewis's view Pound, Eliot, and Joyce did not excite or stimulate), for Wells suggested the notion that mankind can find real education, cheerfulness, kindness, honesty.[23] Lewis went on to reveal what he liked in Wells, in a passage in which he compares Wells and Dickens:

> Humor—passion—devotion to dull but well-loved people—hatred of cruelty—joy in a story for the story's sake and in a phrase for its innocent-seeming kick—Dickens and Wells had them all. If Dickens had the greater inexplicable magic, Wells had the greater knowledge of hidden motives, the deeper comprehension of the world's peril of self-destruction, and infinitely more freedom from sentimentality.

In 1946 after forty years of observing literary and political events, Lewis concludes this eulogy of Wells by saying, "It may be that for us, now, he is the more important of the two novelists—which might leave only Tolstoy and Dostoevsky on higher thrones." Lewis's enthusiasm seems to have had no bounds. He named his first child "Wells Lewis"; he dedicated *The Innocents* to Wells (among others); he was eager to have Wells's opinion of his novels; in England he sought out Wells's company and later remembered with joy his intimate contacts with his mentor.[24]

The novels by Wells that the young Lewis liked best were *The History of Mr. Polly* and *Tono-Bungay*, but he had also read *The Wheels of Chance, Kipps,* and *Love and Mr. Lewisham.* These, let it be noted, are not Wells's books of science fiction but are novels of the road; they are quixotic adventures, wayfaring tales, quests for a princess, and stories of reform. In his foreword to *Polly*, Lewis said that he has found the book "as contagious a comedy as ever—the eternal story of the kind, imaginative, friendly Little Man, whose heart and courage would anywhere . . . lift him from behind the counter of the Gents' Furnishings Shoppe, and lead him out to find a wayside world that is perpetually new and surprising."[25] Lewis's five apprentice books show the powerful influence of Wells upon him. His first novel, *Our Mr. Wrenn,* is all Wells—not only in the similarity of the names Polly, Kipps, and Wrenn, and in their timidity and yearnings and adventures as Little Men, but also in the books' commentaries on education, business, and the social order.[26] Lewis said that *Tono-Bungay* had a greater influence on him than any other work of fiction he ever read.

The gaiety, the zest for life, and the reformist ideas of Wells were what appealed to Lewis and struck harmony with the romantic mood of the years after his graduation from Yale. The inspiration of the literary life as well as the desire to see the world had led him, after several short-term newspaper jobs, to take the position of part-time secretary to Grace MacGowan Cooke at Carmel, California. There Lewis got to know Jack London, a socialist and a scoffer at the effete East, of which Henry James was taken to be the epitome. From that time Lewis remembered an amusing occasion on which Jack London read from James: "Jack picked up James's *The Wings of the Dove* and, standing there, short, burly, in soft shirt and black tie, the Master read aloud in a bewildered way while Henry James's sliding, slithering, glittering verbiage unwound itself on and on. Jack banged the book down and wailed, 'Do any of you know what all this junk is about?' " Lewis explained the meaning of the performance as "the clash between Main Street and Beacon Street that is eternal in American culture."[27] In Lewis's view, the Easterners were "genteel" and the Westerners were "authentic" (that didn't mean that Lewis could resist dressing like and seeking the company of Easterners).

Among the writers to whom Lewis gave allegiance—Wells, London, and Dreiser—"style" meant finickiness. "Who cares for fine style!" shouted Frank Norris. "Tell your yarn and let your style go to the devil. We don't want literature, we want life."[28] Dreiser, Lewis said in his Nobel Prize speech, is an author who gives us rich life, yet the effete critics would say that Dreiser's style is cumbersome, that his choice of words is insensitive, that he is therefore unworthy of the prize himself. "I am not exactly sure what this mystic quality 'style' may be," Lewis said, "but I find the word so often in the writings of minor critics that I suppose it must exist."[29] Indeed, Thomas K. Whipple made what remains the sharpest indictment of Lewis's own style:

> His manner is founded on the best uses of salesmanship, publicity, and advertising. It is heavily playful and vivacious, highly and crudely colored, brisk and snappy. . . . His people do not run, they "gallop"; instead of speaking, they "warble" or "gurgle" or "carol"; commonplace folk are "vanilla-flavored"; interior decorators are "daffodilic young men," "achingly well-dressed"; dancing becomes "the refined titillations of communal embracing."[30]

Nor can one often find in Lewis beauties of style consonant with the subject matter that demands them. Sherwood Anderson saw in the texture of Lewis's prose "but faint joy," leading him to wonder whether Lewis had found little pleasure either in life itself or in his effort to create art.[31] But perhaps Lewis really had a style suitable to his purpose—a style for billboards and warning signs. He disliked pretension and saw no need for experimentation. He had chosen to scold the present, not carve new paths into the future. He had harsh words for those writers whose styles would require close attention from elitist critics. Henry James, Gertrude Stein, and James Joyce all came in for his disapproval, along with lesser writers whom Lewis called "pious manurists" and accused of displaying "the coy snootiness of obscurity."[32] Yet language was his greatest preoccupation. It could hold and give expression to all that he hated. He gave his energies to parodying the false styles of preachers, politicians, advertisers, editorialists.

In this account of influences from Lewis's reading, we must take note of H. L. Mencken, an adventurer against sentimentalism. Mencken's ideas are traceable in the articles Lewis wrote in the twenties, and his views of literary history and literary criticism appear in Lewis's Nobel Prize speech, some ten or perhaps twenty years after Mencken had enunciated them. In the literary and social history of the twenties that has been brilliantly spread before us by Frederick J. Hoffman, Lewis has his place with Mencken and George Jean Nathan.[33] It is to other chapters that Eliot, Hemingway, and Fitzgerald belong. Lewis chose to make his fiction out of criticism of the middle class. Others chose to transmute into art the wounds of the war, the loss of innocence, or the Southern past.

Mencken's targets were the Middlewest, the hinterland, the Bible belt, and clergy, Rotarians, and politicians. Lewis, independently, had tried attacking such targets in scattered sketches embedded within his early romantic fiction. But in *Main Street* he attacked all—the villages, the small businessmen, the preachers, the church ladies, the politicians. His program and Mencken's were much alike. He was eager for Mencken to see and review his work, and putting forth one of his promotional schemes, he wrote to his publisher to list Mencken with those who were to receive notices about the new book. When a congratulatory note arrived from Mencken, Lewis exclaimed, "Luck!"[34] Mencken wrote enthusiastic reviews of both *Main Street* and *Babbitt.* He said of *Elmer Gantry:* "The story is beautifully designed, and it moves with the inevitability of a fugue. It is packed with observation, all fresh, all shrewd, all sound."[35]

In Lewis's Nobel Prize Address, an important document in his attempt to purge gentility, we find many of Mencken's ideas of literary history. Lewis announced that "the great Cambridge-Concord circle of the middle of the Nineteenth Century—Emerson, Longfellow, Lowell, Holmes, the Alcotts—were sentimental reflections of Europe, and they left no school, no influence."[36] He went on to say that "Whitman and Thoreau and Poe and, in some degree, Hawthorne, were outcasts, men alone and despised, berated by the New Humanists of their generation." He wanted to see an American standard of literature, but he said that "it was with the emergence of William Dean Howells that we first began to have something like a standard, and a very bad standard it was." His treatment of Howells, however, was unfair, for, though he acknowledged that "Mr. Howells was one of the gentlest, sweetest, and most honest of men," he adds that Howells "had the code of a pious old maid whose greatest delight was to have tea at the vicarage." (Mencken had written of "the tea-party niceness of Howells.") Lewis went on: Howells had a "fantastic vision of life, which he innocently conceived to be realistic," for in it "the farmer must never be covered with muck, the seaman must never roll out bawdy chanteys, the factory-hand must be thankful to his good employer." Lewis echoed the notion that Howells had tamed Mark Twain and Hamlin Garland. Garland himself, under Howells's influence, dropped from a "harsh and magnificent realist into a genial and insignificant lecturer." Meanwhile, there were "surly and authentic fellows" at work: "Whitman and Melville, then Dreiser and James Huneker and Mencken." His list still confuses romantic, realist, and esthete. Yet one sees Lewis's desire in 1930 to be associated with a new group of "authentic" writers—including promising young novelists such as Hemingway, Wolfe, Wilder, Dos Passos, and Faulkner.

As to the situation in American literature in general, he has a complaint: "In America most of us—not readers alone but even writers—are still afraid of any literature which is not a glorification of everything American." To be loved, our writers must assert "that all American men are tall, handsome, rich, honest, and powerful at golf"; that country towns are full of kindly people; that American girls become perfect mothers; that New York contains only millionaires; that the West is still heroic and the South is a plantation of moonlight and magnolias. Here he resurrected his enemy once more—the stereotypes he felt he was fighting against. "The American novelist or poet or dramatist or sculptor or painter must work alone, in confusion, unassisted save by his own integrity." A writer "is expected by his readers to be only a decorator or a clown. . . . And he has no institution, no group, to which he can turn for inspiration, whose criticism he can accept and whose praise will be precious to him." (Is this a reaction to his own fifteen wandering and painful apprentice years? And does it reflect his isolation from the expatriate writers of the twenties, who knew each other and communicated with and helped each other, even if at times they envied one another?)

The last letter from Mencken is sad to read. The occasion is the publication of *Cass Timberlane* in 1945. Mencken says that the book is not so good as *Babbitt* or *Gantry*, but that it is the best Lewis has done since *Dodsworth*. He tells Lewis that the country "swarms" with subjects for him. He presses Lewis toward satire and realism. He lists "the rich radical, the bogus expert, the numskull newspaper proprietor (or editor), the career jobholder, the lady publicist, the crooked (or, more usually, idiotic) labor leader, the press agent, and so on."[37]

Wells and Mencken were as close as Lewis came to having living models and advisers. They helped him to be an adventurer, encouraged his capacity to pit observation against fancy, and emboldened him to undertake big subjects in an audacious way. But their names indicate why Lewis felt apart from the newest currents of the late twenties and oncoming thirties. He had constructed a successful career, which meant fighting his way clear, if he could, of some harrowing literary shackles. Yet he was not completely free. Old inhibitions constrained him.

Throughout this account of Lewis's struggle to find appropriate modes of writing and to place himself within a literary tradition, one figure who might have helped seems barely visible. Mark Twain had enacted a drama like the one Lewis was enacting, and his life and work might have been a model for Lewis. Mark Twain's emancipation from Samuel Clemens is, in fact, realism's victory over romance—though hardly a complete or permanent triumph, and one scored with much pain. Mark Twain fictionalized it in Tom Sawyer and Huck Finn. Tom's mind is filled with A-rabs, ransoms, coats-of-arms, Lady Jane Grey, and romance by-the-book; Huck's is attentive to a Barlow knife, candlestick, tin cup, and fish-line—the practical artifacts of common sense. But to his most important American predecessor, Lewis seems to have given less attention than he gave to those writers who early stimulated the romantic impulses within him.

Chapter 3

Adventure

As we have noted, Lewis's journey ended alone. In his youth, however, hope, eagerness, and exuberance illuminated his life, just as isolation darkened it. Wanderlust was an outlet for that dreamy boy in the prairie village who read widely in romance—in Scott, Kipling, Irving, and Tennyson, and in Howard Pyle's retelling of the Arthurian legends. His heart yearned for *elsewhere.* Far from worrying about roots then, he wanted very much to get away. Elsewhere there were lovely places and beautiful women. Elsewhere there were adventures and worlds to conquer. The metaphor of medieval romance cast its spell upon him as a boy and seems to have remained within him in maturity. He sought elsewhere, where his fancy impelled him, yet he remembered the "fallacy of elsewhere" and countered with realistic observation. Drawing from Lewis's essays and fiction, what I offer here is a composite picture of the lands of elsewhere that Lewis invaded and caused his characters to invade over a period of almost fifty years.

In 1900, it is true, young men who left the villages to attend college or conquer the cities could look forward to stimulating events: muckrakers and reformers attacked abuses, women demanded their rights, and Europe's culture beckoned. A footloose youth might sweep back and forth across the nation, eastward to Europe and southward to Panama, and then dream of China and India. So Lewis did, and so his wandering heroes do in his apprentice novels about "elsewhere" by which he learned his craft: following the trail of the hawk in the adventure of adventure itself, or breathing the free, exhilarating, regenerating air of the western roads that led to the Pacific, or seeking love and fame. Hawk Ericson, Milt Daggett, Claire Boltwood—he sent forth these vagabonds in his books as embodiments of optimism and innocence.

Yet the story of Lewis's career must always bring us back to the American Middlewest; of his twenty-two novels, all but six involve midwestern protagonists or midwestern locales. Discussing the importance of scene in fiction, Lewis wrote, "The scene of a story is the environment affecting the character, and . . . is as much a part of the protagonist's character and development as his heart."[1] What Lewis said of fictional creations was equally true of himself. The scenes of Lewis's novels might be a village or New York or New England or Europe, cities of seventy thousand or three hundred thousand or millions; all of them he strove to know well, for it was a foundation of his method that one should write of a place only when he had gotten to know it "by the ten thousand unconscious experiences which come from living in it."[2] To supply the setting for his fictions, he committed himself to observation and research.

The locale that he knew best was the Middlewest, and the scene that went heart-deep was the midwestern village of a few thousand persons, the kind of village in which he was born and reared. "It is extraordinary how deep is the impression made by the place of one's birth and rearing, and how lasting are its memories," he wrote some twenty-nine years after leaving Sauk Centre to go east to college.[3] "In this more than a quarter of a century, I have been back two or three times for a couple of months, several times for a couple of weeks, but otherwise I have been utterly out of touch with the town. Yet it is as vivid to my mind as though I had left there yesterday."

The small town had a long arm, he said. He claimed that Sauk Centre occupied his thinking—haunted him—for some fifteen years during which he was searching for a way of understanding and explaining it. Lewis believed that understanding Sauk Centre meant understanding much of America, for the Main Street of Sauk Centre (or of its fictional counterpart, Gopher Prairie) was, as he insisted in the preface to *Main Street*, "the continuation of Main Streets everywhere." In another essay, he wrote that "to understand America, it is merely necessary to understand Minnesota. But to understand Minnesota you must be an historian, an ethnologist, a poet, a cynic, and a graduate prophet all in one."[4] Indeed, in order to know America, Lewis did try each of those roles at some time: he tried to be historian of the pioneer spirit that settled Minnesota; ethnologist of its racial and social make-up; poet of romantic love, of the joys of rural childhood, and of the consolations of field and lake; cynical piercer of the façade that covered the bitter realities of American life; and recorder of new attitudes and achievements.

The Minnesota which he adjured us to understand fascinated

Lewis. In 1923 he wrote the essay about it which indicates the view he wanted the public to have of the setting of his boyhood and the background of his novels. He would try to picture it accurately, but inevitably elements of selection and subjectivity prevent our receiving the whole truth about the place. One sees him trying to suggest a myth in broad and romantic strokes, a vision of pioneerland which seems the twin image of his other effort to portray the times in medieval terms. When one reads his description of the people of Minnesota, one suspects that Sinclair Lewis, not God, was their creator. (In 1949 he will write a historical novel about the origin of the people and place.) Lewis begins by recording the incredible newness of the state: "Before 1837, there were less than three hundred whites and mixed breeds in all this Minnesotan domain of eighty thousand square miles."[5] He praises Minnesota's rolling prairies and lovely lakes. Beyond the plains country, there is a northern pine wilderness, the Big Woods—a land of lumber camps, Indians, tote-roads, and Paul Bunyan.

But it is the people most of all who must be understood. Racially, "in most of the State there is a predomination of Yankees, Germans, Irish, and all branches of Scandinavians, Icelanders and Danes as well as Swedes and Norwegians," who, Lewis notes regretfully, far from being comic and alien stereotypes, Americanize all too quickly. Parts of the state are raw, but in the cities and in a few of the towns "there is as firm a financial oligarchy and almost as definite a social system as London, and this power is behind all Sound Politics, in direct or indirect control of all business. It has its Old Families, who tend to marry only within their set." Some grandchildren of the pioneers are anything but carriers of the pioneer spirit: they are tearoom habitués and Pierce-Arrow owners. "Naturally, beneath this Junker class there is a useful, sophisticated, and growing company of doctors, teachers, newspapermen, liberal lawyers, musicians. . . . There is a scientific body of farmers. . . . And still more naturally, between Labor and Aristocracy there is an army of the peppy, poker-playing, sales-hustling He-men who are our most characteristic Americans." The list sounds like the cast for the Sinclair Lewis novels; his essay is, however, social science as he sees it.

To understand Lewis the man and the controlling ideas and emotions of his work, especially as they come out in his portraits of villagers, it is useful to look at the way his perception of the hometown changed. His new attitude toward the town—his critical and aloof attitude, his disillusionment, and his keener comprehension of its realities—forms the basis of that central phase of Lewis's development which he expressed fictionally in Carol Kennicott's antagonism toward Gopher Prairie. Two influences mark Lewis's change of view: his reading and his return to the hometown after two years of experience away from it. Garland and Dreiser especially released him, he said, so that, whatever the townspeople thought themselves to be or pretended to be, he had license to see them freely and portray them as they truly were.

Back in 1905, he recalled, a literary view of village life persisted which he clearly, though perhaps passively, shared. It was the widely held picture of the village as a paradise of white homes under green trees. Neighborliness was the glory of the town. "In the cities, nobody knew or cared; but back home, the Neighbors were one great big jolly family. They lent you money, without questioning, to send Ed to business college; they soothed your brow in sickness—dozens of them . . . ; and when you had nevertheless passed beyond, they sat up with your corpse and your widow. Invariably they encouraged youth to go to bigger and nobler things." Such was the myth recreated in dozens of books which fed the quixotic illusion of village life. But another view in fiction was beginning to develop which opened his eyes. In 1905 "I returned to my Minnesota village for vacation after my Sophomore year in Yale, and . . . after two months of overhearing the villagers none too softly wonder, 'Why don't Doc Lewis make Harry get a job on a farm instead of letting him sit around readin' and readin' a lot of fool histories and God knows what all?' I was converted to the faith that a good deal of this Neighborliness was a fake."[6] Neighborliness a fake—that was the overwhelming insight he says he gained that summer, even if it was to take him fifteen years more to examine it and to express its meaning in artistic form. The scene of a story, he had said, is the environment affecting character, but neither village scene nor the persons of the village were what they had appeared to be or had been represented as being in fiction. Out of this visit and several others, especially one with Grace Hegger Lewis, his bride from the East, came the attitude which controls most of *Main Street,* that of the "alien cynic" (as he calls himself in the preface) who finds so much of village life a sham.

Gopher Prairie, Joralemon, Panama, Wheatsylvania, Waubanakee, Black Thread Center—these are Lewis's fictional towns, and each bears down on the heart of his protagonists. Yet beyond the towns lie mountains and fields. He strained to give his descriptions of nature an inspirational quality, as if to inscribe upon his protagonists' imaginations formative and indelible ideals. Hawk Ericson, in *The Trail of the Hawk,* is the first to feel the imprint of nature.[7] He glanced at Joralemon Lake: "The surface of the water was smooth, and tinted like a bluebell, save for one patch in the current where wavelets leaped with October madness in sparkles of diamond fire. Across the lake, woods sprinkled with gold-dust and paprika broke the sweep of sparse yellow stubble, and a red barn was softly brilliant in the caressing sunlight and lively air of the Minnesota prairie" (p. 4). Later Hawk wanders through a "gipsy day" on which "the sun rolled splendidly through the dry air, over miles of wheat stubble, whose gray-yellow prickles were transmuted by distance into tawny velvet" (p. 30). In *Main Street,* Carol's mind has fed on such scenes of the countryside, too. To her vision she adds what her fancy wants to see. So she feels the shock of discovery of the reality of the town most deeply. Riding toward Gopher Prairie, Carol is startled by the sight of other villages along the way. When the train stops in Schoenstrom, a hamlet of a hundred and fifty inhabitants, she sees no activity other than the station agent hoisting a dead calf aboard the train. The business-center was simply "a row of one-story shops covered with galvanized iron, or with clapboards painted red and bilious yellow." She is distressed by the sight of these ill-assorted, temporary-looking buildings, the one-room station, the mirey cattle-pen, and the crimson wheat-elevator, with its cupola on the ridge of a shingled roof, resembling "a broad-shouldered man with a small, vicious, pointed head" (p. 23). As she comes into Gopher Prairie, a town of three thousand people, she sees that it is "merely an enlargement of all the hamlets which they had been passing. . . . It was unprotected and unprotecting; there was no dignity in it nor any hope of greatness" (p. 26).

These are by no means the quaint, picturesque villages that literature had taught her to expect. Where are the lovely houses, the large green trees, the fresh prairie breezes, the silvery pastors, the honest yeoman? Instead of them, she finds a town which Lewis describes as hot, dusty, soggy, parched, cramped, and nauseating. Her new home seems to her smug, damp, sickly, dried, cheap, dingy, lugubrious, airless, dismal, and gravelike, while in her room the chair squeaks: "choke her—choke her—smother her" (p. 31). The literary tradition of the Midwest had done much to mislead her; the picture presented by books is untrue.

The central image of *Main Street* is Carol's walk about the town on the day of her arrival. Designed to challenge the traditional descriptions of lovely villages, it employs such adjectives as muddy, grasping, unclean, rickety, oozing, greasy, curdled, pawed-over, faded, sleazy, broken, and raw:

> When Carol had walked for thirty-two minutes she had completely covered the town, east and west, north and south; and she stood at the corner of Main Street and Washington Avenue and despaired.
>
> Main Street with its two-story brick shops, its story-and-a-half wooden residences, its muddy expanse from concrete walk to walk, its huddle of Fords and lumber-wagons, was too small to absorb her. The broad, straight, unenticing gashes of the streets let in the grasping prairie on every side. She realized the vastness and the emptiness of the land. The skeleton iron windmill on the farm a few blocks away, at the north end of Main Street, was like the ribs of a dead cow. She thought of the coming of the Northern winter, when the unprotected houses would crouch together in terror of storms galloping out of the wild waste. They were so small and weak, the little brown houses. They were shelters for sparrows, not homes for warm laughing people (p. 33).

To combat the ugliness, Carol wished to build beautiful homes and a Georgian courthouse; she would plant flowers and trees; she would change the environment which somehow both is created by and creates the villagers. But she is thwarted. Dullness, drabness, and sameness rule. In her test of the environment, the environment fails her. She is not alone in her attitudes, however. She is but one of many men and women, Lewis said, who are dissatisfied, rebellious, bewildered, and defeated in the village.

With *Main Street*, Lewis felt himself launched upon a new phase of his career. Having in his apprentice work already touched upon village, city, metropolis, and foreign nation as environments, he went over the ground again more carefully and perceptively in the succeeding ten years, armed with new generalizations, some of which he had discovered by his own adventure into each locale, and some of which he had taken over from Wells, Van Wyck Brooks, Veblen, and Mencken. He felt with Wells, for instance, that the small men of business who run the government and dictate the culture should be exposed in their smallness. He was influenced by Brooks in thinking that there was a warfare between the acquisitive and the creative instincts. He agreed with critics who wrote in Harold Stearns's symposium that businessmen were essentially dishonest, that universities provided no education, that America offered her writers and scientists only entrapment and hostility.[8] The new America, of which Minnesota itself had been an example, had leapt too fast from potatoes to Proust. The America of a hundred and twenty million people cannot be as simple and as pastoral as it once was. All too many magazine writers still "chanted" that "the relationships between father and son, between husband and wife, are precisely the same in an apartment in a thirty-story palace today, with three motor cars awaiting the family below and five books on the library shelves and a divorce imminent in the family next week, as were those relationships in a rose-veiled five-room cottage in 1880."[9] In short, America had gone through a revolutionary change from rustic colony to world empire, and the fiction of its writers must show it. His fiction, consequently, would be set against a background of this too-rapid but fascinating change.

Many of Lewis's characters spend their whole lives in villages, but many others simply start there and then wander forth. Sharpening his perceptions on the socialism of Wells and the iconoclasm of Mencken, Lewis turned his attention from the villages and towns to the "Zeniths." Their effect upon personality was equally stultifying. These cities of about 350,000 people, though industrially magnificent, though importers of Galsworthy, Caruso, and Kreisler, are yet villages: "Villages—overgrown towns—three-quarters of a million people still dressing, eating, building houses, attending church, to make an impression on their neighbors, quite as they did back on Main Street, in villages of two thousand."[10] Not yet cultivated metropolises, these are the communities "in between," which have grown too fast. They are all much the same: if you were by magic taken instantly to any of them and set down in the business center, "in a block, say, with a new hotel, a new motion-picture theater, and a line of newish shops, not three hours of the intensest study of the passing people . . . would indicate in what city, indeed in what part of the country, you were." All such cities and all their inhabitants have "cast off all the hard-earned longings of mankind and joined in a common aspiration to be rich, notorious, and One Hundred Per Cent American." Here, as in the thesis of *Main Street,* we have the heart of Lewis's social criticism, for which his venturing characters are illustrations, examples, proofs. The city of Zenith itself, for instance, aspires "above the morning mist"; it is a city "built—it seemed—for giants." But, we are at once told, "there was nothing of the giant in the aspect of the man who was beginning to awaken"—George F. Babbitt—nor in the aspects of his small-minded, dull, bickering, dishonest, and discontented family and friends.

Yet a great metropolis like New York is no better than a Zenith. For Lewis's eager romantics, who set out to conquer the city, New York is wonderful but overpowering. His youths arrive in New York to assume their clerkships and then to succeed in the world of business, but soon the atmosphere of the city has subdued them and they cry for companionship. His short stories tell about their woes over and over again. His novel of mid-career, *Dodsworth,* supplies an extensive analysis of the city. Samuel Dodsworth returns from Europe with the expectation of taking pleasure in the sight of America. From the ship he is awed by the vision of New York: "High up shone the towers and spires of an enchanted city floating upon the mist, pyramids and domes glistening in the early sun, vast walls studded with golden windows, spellbound and incredible" (p. 154). But soon he is walking the hot side streets, which he finds appallingly dirty, with flying newspapers, piles of bottles and rags and manure and the "summertime stench of rotten bananas, unwashed laundry, ancient bedding, and wet pavements" (p. 156). It was, Sam feels, "a city nervous as a thwarted woman. . . . It seemed so masculine in its stalwart buildings, but there was nothing masculine in its heat-shocked, clamor-maddened nerves." He then realizes that New York provides every necessity "save a place, a café or a plaza or a not-too-lady-like tea-shop, in which he could sit and be human" (p. 163). His friend, the newspaperman Ross Ireland, cries out, "It's the dirtiest, noisiest, craziest hole I was ever in! I hate it" (p. 158). Young Lewis, too, had come hopefully to New York. It bustled with diverse races which excited him and which he tried to portray, though never successfully. New York had its advantages: "It is the most exciting, idea-jammed, high-colored city in the world, except perhaps Moscow."[11] But the New York of his fiction—of his emotions, one might say—is drawn more in disgust than in wonder. Late in life Lewis summed up in his diary his ultimate attitude toward New Yorkers: "a distressful and neurotic people."[12]

Europe, however, where Lewis travelled so much, offered a last choice of "elsewhere" in which life might be worth living. England is the country Lewis first visited, attracted by the fiction of Scott and Dickens. It is where Lewis's first hero, William Wrenn, ventures, but Wrenn is all wonder and no mind. In *Dodsworth* there is much analysis of the quality of life in Europe. European cities have the cafés where one can relax, they have the good talk, they have an authentic sense of the past, they have edifices like Notre Dame Cathedral, where Dodsworth finds "strength and endurance and wisdom" (p. 141). Europe also has its countryside and its villas. In such countryside near Naples the discontented Sam Dodsworth, speechless with wonder, feels stirring within him a restoration to meaningful life. The Italian peasant, he is told by Edith Cortright, "loves earth and sun and wind and rain." The Tyrolese, the Prussian, the Frenchman, the Englishman—they love the earth, as no American does. "That's the strength of Europe—not its so-called 'culture,' its galleries and neat voices and knowledge of languages, but its nearness to earth." She continues her analysis: "And that's the weakness of America—not its noisiness and its cruelty and its cinema vulgarity but the way in which it erects steel-and-glass skyscrapers and miraculous cement-and-glass factories and tiled kitchens and wireless antennae and popular magazines to insulate it from the good vulgarity of earth!" (p. 360). Thus, Lewis's fictional testing of environments suggests that as place bears in upon one's heart, the European closeness to earth offers a salvation which should be sought in America as well, where only the pioneers had known it. Post-pioneer America had destroyed its land. Its buildings are ugly beyond forgiveness.

To say that Lewis the wanderer returned home again to Minnesota is to flirt with a cliché. In fact, his efforts to live there in the forties failed as much as did his efforts to live anywhere else for any extended period of time. After leaving Minnesota for the last time in 1946, Lewis tried living in Massachusetts, then went abroad.

It would be sentimental to suggest that Lewis was spiritually at home only in Minnesota, yet it does seem true that certain values and attitudes of the Midwest remained strong within him. He remembered and exaggerated the good times of his youth. From the village he was pleased to think that he carried such standards as Ann Vickers inherits from her father in a midwest environment:

> Sobriety, honest work, paying his debts, loyalty to his mate and to his friends, disdain of unearned rewards—he once refused a tiny legacy from an uncle whom he had despised—and a pride that would let him neither cringe nor bully, these were her father's code, and in a New York where spongers and sycophants and gayly lying people, pretty little people, little playing people, were not unknown even among social workers and scientists, that code haunted her (*Ann Vickers*, pp. 7–8).

Lewis believed in (and always tried to practice) a similar code: to value romance, to honor the pioneer, to pay one's debts, to respect the social conscience of populism and the optimism of progressivism, to work hard, and to seek whatever consolation new places can offer. His characters speak with the voice of the Midwest, derived from his experience of listening to the "normal daily drone" of what were to him "the most fascinating and exotic people in the world—the Average Citizens of the United States."[13] For he had heard both the oratory of the circuit and the banal chatter of the Pullman car, the hotel porch, and the dining room table. His best novels—*Main Street, Babbitt, Arrowsmith,* and *Dodsworth*—dealt with Midwesterners and involved him in an attempt to expunge crudity and hypocrisy from midwestern ways and to exalt honor and creativity.

Yet the task was difficult—perhaps impossible. Each man's America is his own, and no one succeeds fully in the effort to understand and explain all of it. Whatever powers a writer might possess, in his attempt to deal with that gigantic, diverse, and intractable material that is America, some defect of vision, narrowness of background, prejudice of feeling might lead him to a kind of failure. Lewis was predisposed to such a fanciful way of seeing that he had to research every item of environment, custom, and personage in order to keep within the bounds of reality. Nonetheless, his vision had been so aslant that it was a lucky moment when he chose caricature, exaggeration, and humor as his modes, thereby sidestepping the imperatives of realism and leaving himself latitude in the recreation of places and persons. To do him justice we should read him with that latitude; it explains his anger and comedy.

What Lewis accomplished was to expose and satirize defects of contemporary manners, stopping at no geographic boundary. He mapped out his own state, which he peopled and then pummelled in his fierce passion to reform. He created several memorable characters symbolic of a confused American era. He vividly pictured them hugging their possessions, desiring to be home yet to be elsewhere, and displaying their disoriented, contradictory, and romantic beliefs. Many of his major and minor figures are involved in significant ways with the Middlewest, and all, like their author, struggle with mixed feelings about the locale of their youth, no matter how far away from it they may be. Personality and place are inevitably entwined. The creed of "elsewhere" may have its fallacy, but travel, adventures, and quests were necessary to Lewis the quixote and to his quixotic characters.

Chapter 4

Enchantment

Enchantment is the result of the transforming power of the imagination. Enchantment nourishes itself on books—on poems of ideality, on popular romantic fiction, on vagabond novels. It draws upon stereotypes within such literature. Preoccupation with stereotypes was strong in Lewis, the result perhaps of his youthful romanticism and his country-boy approach to the larger world. The dreaming mind, filled more with characters out of books than with observations from life, is shocked by its confrontation with reality. Lewis confessed that as a youth he had longed for the lost knights of Minnesota. He was unable to see his townsfolk "really" until he had been shown how to do it by Hamlin Garland.

Lewis recounted an incident which shows the way his mind operated amidst stereotypes and real observations. (Whether the incident occurred this way or not, it remains indicative of his attitudes.) It was supposed to have happened while he was working as a newspaperman in San Francisco (he was about twenty-five years old at the time). He was told that a Chinese prince had just landed, and Lewis "skipped" happily to the hotel to interview him. On the way he planned his story "which would obviously be very funny." The prince would be fat and waddling, with comic mustachios and a long saber, and he would say "Me heapee biggee princee." But Lewis never did see *that* prince. At the door of the suite he was greeted by "a slim Chinaman in morning coat, quite the suavest and coldest and best-spoken man [he] had ever met, with an Oxford accent and a Mayfair blankness." The Chinaman murmured, "It would be quite impossible for you to see His Highness, but I should be glad to answer any questions." Lewis was astounded. He comments: "Questions? I don't think I had any, beyond the familiar 'Huh?' It was a moment of revelation about the world."[1]

Yet the anecdote leaves doubt that this revelation taught Lewis a basic lesson. He continued to fancy a stereotype. Even later in life he would approach a closed door with the image of the kind of person he would meet beyond it. When the door opened, Lewis would find his stereotype shattered—but usually by a figure constructed of qualities at an opposite extreme. He would stare in amazement that human nature could offer up such surprises. What he failed to realize was that he had now placed in the door an image that was often no less a stereotype than the figure his fancy had originally prepared for him to meet: his Oxford Chinese is, after all, no more real than a "heapee biggee" one (a Chinese who talks a pseudo-Indian dialect anyway). The worst result of this way of viewing was his use of this "truth" in serious contexts; the best was to convert it to the exaggerations of American humor.

Two anecdotes that corroborate the strength of his fanciful stereotyping appear in a reminiscence Frances Perkins related to Professor Schorer. Seeing two girls at the ferry house on Staten Island, Lewis imagined that their innocence was in danger and insisted on protecting them; but finally one told him to leave them alone—he was ruining their evening's business. Immediately thereafter, Lewis followed a sick-looking girl to protect her from her male companion who he believed had doped her; but again his fancy received its rebuff when the annoyed woman explained that she had a dizzying headache and her husband was trying to take her home.[2] Such revelations about life, then, were difficult to learn.

Lewis's Foreword to *Angel Pavement* by J. B. Priestley illustrates again how his fanciful imagination would gambol some thirty years later, only to be abruptly "corrected" by his sense of reality. He writes, "To the average American, half of the map of England is filled with baronial estates at which, every week-end, gather a flawed beauty, a well-spoken chauffeur, and nine assorted guests, three of them bearded Levantines and one a psychiatrist with a monocle."[3] Meanwhile, "the other half of the map of England is occupied by a London composed solely of Scotland Yard, Buckingham Palace, the Houses of Parliament, sixty hotels. . . ." For the literate reader there may also be "the tomb of Wordsworth, flint churches, benevolent vicars and malevolent squires, and rustics who chew straws. . . ." The cause of these misconceptions is too much reading of the minor novelists. But, Lewis says, Mr. Priestley writes about real English people, "precisely the sort of people whom we know in offices in Manhattan or Minneapolis or Memphis": the head of the firm, the ambitious typist, the patient chief clerk, and "the jumpy office boy who wants to be a great detective." Lewis has moved from one set of stereotypes to another.

Lewis's courtship of Grace Livingstone Hegger from 1912 to 1914 (his age was twenty-seven to twenty-nine) was characterized by much of the romantic-medieval state of mind. Their hikes and picnics appear in *The Trail of the Hawk* and find parallels in Mrs. Lewis's memoir *With Love from Gracie.* In the memoir, for example, Mrs. Lewis reproduces the following from a note addressed to her in New York:

> To the Hochwohlegeborene Demoiselle,
> The Lady Grace Livingstone Hegger,
> Plesaunce de Château Vieutemps.
> Provence.
> From her servant Francois Villon. . . .

And she reprints a verse from him:

> Please, dear lady, come and play;
> Please don't be industrious,
> Lady, come; let's run away;
> Let's go riding on the bus. . . .

Mrs. Lewis writes of the courtship: "From the beginning he chose for himself the roles of Jacques the Jester and François the Troubadour who sang to the Lady Grace."[4] She says that her copy of *Hawk* is inscribed: "This is not so much a novel, dear, as a record of our games & talks & thoughts and journeys." Of *Main Street, The Trail of the Hawk,* and *Free Air,* Mrs. Lewis states that "in all three books, in varying degrees, I am the chief female character."[5] Describing a trip to France in the mid-twenties, Grace Lewis could still write, "We arrived at Carcassone by moonlight and Jacques the Jester and his Princess of Faraway leaned breathless on the ramparts."[6]

The power of enchantment exerted itself even over the story of his childhood. Later he made some significant adjustments in the account of his early years, as he built what Professor Schorer has called the "official view" of himself. From the time when he achieved success with *Main Street,* Lewis began creating the legend of his life. He reviewed his childhood in Sauk Centre and cast a spell of illusion upon it. He chose to picture this town of two or three thousand persons as a "genuine prairie town, ringed round with wheat fields broken by slew and oak-rimmed lakes, with autumn flight of ducks from Canada."[7] It was, he said, "a shambling prairie village . . . of low wooden shops, of cottages each set in its little garden, of rather fine trees, with the wheat a golden sea for miles about."[8] He proclaimed his boyhood as having been "alarmingly normal," and asserted that his time of youth had possessed qualities missing in later America. As he looked at the sons of rich men in the New England of 1931, with their cars and their travel, it seemed to him that they were not having one-tenth the fun that he had had as a boy, "swimming and fishing in Sauk Lake, or cruising its perilous depths on a raft . . ., tramping out to Fairy Lake for a picnic, tramping ten miles on end, with a shotgun, in October; sliding on Hoboken Hill, stealing melons, or listening to the wonders of an elocutionist at the G.A.R. Hall."[9] In later years nostalgia frequently overcame him: "I find myself thinking of its [Sauk Centre's] streets and its people and the familiar, friendly faces when I am on the great avenues of New York, or Paris, or Berlin, or Stockholm. . . . I am quite certain that I could have been born and reared in no place in the world where I would have had more friendliness." Lewis summed up these happy reminiscences by declaring, "It was a good time, a good place, and a good preparation for life."

But we now know a great deal about Lewis's childhood which he hid from such accounts. The town has benefited from his imagination; it gains from the effects of fancy, the power of enchantment. First of all, in spite of his declarations of an idyllic and innocent boyhood, we need to read only a few more of Lewis's own reminiscences in order to become aware of a self-conscious and defensive, if not contradictory, tone, by means of both an admission and a warning to fend off psychological inquiry into his past. Psychologists, he said, may speak of "literary exhibitionism" as a compensation for a writer's having been outfought, outswum, and outloved in his youth; "of me that explanation must have been partly true, but only partly, because while I was a mediocre sportsman in Boytown, I was neither a cripple nor a Sensitive Soul."[10] "Partly true"—for all was not ideal in Boytown. A biographical article by Christian Gauss concerning those years has as its theme Lewis's hurt and resentment.[11] For instance, Lewis was frozen out of a Robin Hood Club he had organized (the boys "decided he was queer," we are told). Suggestions confirming hurts and defeats appear, humorously enough, even in Lewis's memories of early reading; as a kid brother, Harry was a nuisance to his older brother Claude and the gang, who mocked his vocabulary and elaborately evaded his company. Having failed to startle them at sports, young Lewis decided that he would overwhelm Claude's gang with "strictly high-class intellectual feats!" He undertook a resolution: "All right, then I'd become a reporter, and *then* they'd be sorry!"[12] This anecdote offers a tempting simplification of the motive that led him to become a satirist, yet it suggests that early enough he felt the emotions of one who must pay back those who have hurt him. Lewis recalled, furthermore, that the urge to impress the gang may have motivated his reading. He would go home "heartbroken" to read Grote's *History of Greece*, "a vast and horrible opus in many volumes with fine print," which he plodded through, not because he enjoyed it, but because he hoped, "vainly, thus to impress Claude, Jim Hendryx, and the other young intelligentsia of Sauk Centre."[13] If not for this reason alone, but more likely out of the insatiable curiosity that is the mark of the gifted, Lewis read widely. In general, then, the picture Lewis conveyed through self-portraits was not entirely true, as Professor Schorer's researches have proved. It was not an idyllic boyhood. Lewis had few friends; he was awkward and lonely; he could not hunt or swim. Don Quixote invokes enchantments "to rationalize his defeats and embarrassments," says Professor Levin.[14] So did Sinclair Lewis.

Lewis's reminiscences do not tell us much about his parents. He was the third son of Dr. Edwin J. and Emma Kermott Lewis. After Mrs. Lewis's death, Dr. Lewis remarried. Harry was then six years old. Benjamin Stolberg recalled that "Lewis described [his father] to me as 'very dignified, stern, rather soldierly, absolutely honest, and a fair to good country doctor.'" Lewis would speak of his father rarely, "with considerable respect and no affection."[15] Grace Lewis described the doctor as "distinguished looking, tall and spare. . . . A fine forehead above deep-set, considering eyes, a faint smile beneath a close-cropped gray mustache, hard-surfaced pepper-and-salt clothes . . . and a high wide open-in-front starched collar and dark bow-tie."[16] She thought the doctor's second wife plain, though a warmer person. Grace Lewis made her account of the visit of the younger Lewises to Sauk Centre in 1916 the story of the introduction of the eastern bride to the suspicious home-folks. Her picture of Dr. Lewis is that of a narrow, habit-ridden, unbending Puritan. One gathers that her impressions were justified. The doctor would force his family to eat on time to the minute; he compelled the newlyweds to sacrifice their privacy so that cool breezes might sweep through the open bedroom doors at night; he kept the ritual of the Saturday night bath; he scrutinized their mail and their whereabouts. He awoke early and he worked hard.

Grace Lewis offers an additional insight into that family of doctors (for the second brother Claude was by 1916 a physician, too). She tells us that the father, who before becoming a physician had been a schoolmaster, would say to his son, "'Harry, why can't you do like any other boy ought to do?'"[17] According to Gauss, young Lewis knew "that it would be counted against him, even by his father, if he mooned around in the woods all day."[18] Sensitive Souls had no place in pioneerland, where Lewis, occasionally accompanying the doctor on his rounds and closely observing his cool competence, was developing an awe of the person who does his job well and pays his debts responsibly.[19] Lewis would suffer conflict and guilt later when he found it necessary to satirize such a person's dullness. Why, we shall see him asking, need courage and practicality always appear to be conjoined with dullness and coldness in these contradictory men, of whom Dr. Will Kennicott, whose work Carol witnesses, is a most striking fictional example? How could one come to a resolution of one's mingled admiration and disappointment?

In his fiction, Lewis enjoyed creating a variety of ways in which people could turn out to be opposite to the image they initially suggested. In part, he did so because of the romantic way he was predisposed to approach the world. In part, he did so out of playfulness. His shortcomings in handling the basic theme of appearance and reality, however, result from the fact that he generally created characters whose line of vision is outward; they seldom come to such self-knowledge as would reveal their own complicity in creating a world that so disappoints and betrays them.

Thus he played with stereotype and counter-stereotype, and especially in his minor characters delighted in the game of creating boy drunkards who turn out to be conventionally good preachers, or effeminate men who might seem timid or cowardly but turn out to be brave in war. For example, the Klebses, father and son, are the socialist pariahs of Ann Vickers's hometown. Both are outspoken radicals and atheists, but paradoxically they end up opposite to what they seem to promise: "Some day [Adolph, the son] was to be the manager of a fairly good garage in Los Angeles, and Oscar to sleep irritably in the Catholic Cemetery of Waubanakee, Illinois."[20]

It often seems that Lewis is shouting at the reader (and perhaps at the homefolks): "Don't jump to conclusions: the good will be bad and the bad will be good; the fast will be slow and the slow will be fast." There are several Oxonian Chinese Indians in Lewis's work, and there are a good many characters who emerge from fantasies of other kinds.

His imagination would drift to strange Samarkands. For example, when Lewis decided that the notion of a pure blood-line was simply a poor excuse for prejudice, he began giving major and minor characters elaborate family trees, including as many diverse branches as his fancy could think of in what he believed to be humorous juxtapositions. Sweeney Fishberg is the clearest example of this, though Barney Dolphin of *Ann Vickers* is another. Fishberg is the German-Irish-Jewish lawyer in *Cass Timberlane* and *Kingsblood Royal* who is both honest and crooked, both gruff and gentle, both crude and cultured:

> Sweeney Fishberg was perhaps the most remarkable man in the cosmos of Grand Republic and surrounding terrain.
>
> He was an attorney, of liberal tastes, equally likely to take a labor-union case for nothing or to take the most fraudulent of damage suits for a contingent fee which, to the fury of his Yankee wife, he was likely to give to a fund for strikers—any strikers on any strike. He was a saint and a shyster; part Jewish and part Irish and part German; he had once acted in a summer stock company and once taught Greek in a West Virginia college; he was a Roman Catholic, and a mystic who bothered his priest with metaphysical questions; he was in open sympathy with the Communist Party.
>
> . . . No lawyer in the district ever brought such doubtful suits into court, yet no lawyer was more decorous, more co-operative with the judge.[21]

This has about it the view of the quixote—that is, it is a creature of fancy. But in such characterization by opposites, the gap between extremes remains unexplained and undramatized—and we wonder what the opposites mean, how the character reconciles the opposites, what conflicts the opposites bring, how so many opposites became fixed in one personality. Lewis answered none of these questions because he felt that the extreme grotesquerie of linked opposites was comic in the broadest sense, and thus self-justifying. His motive may have been an earthy (though tasteless and certainly anti-semitic) joke. Taking a Jew and marrying him to an Irish girl, Lewis calls the offspring Sweeney Fishberg. Then he marries Sweeney to a Protestant and converts him to Catholicism. Since Fishberg has mixed heritage, he will be a shyster, yet somehow also a man of principle. For the last stroke, Lewis makes the Catholic sympathetic to communism. The sketch has the extravagance of frontier humor, but a dozen stereotyped strokes do not release insight into character.

In *Elmer Gantry,* where Lewis shows us a vast gallery of preachers, his fancy delighted in playing with exotics who combine opposite qualities. One is the Reverend Andrew Pengilly. In previous novels Lewis had worked hard to prove that the silvery-haired pastor of the idealized stories of small town life was unreal. Now he tries to reverse himself. "If you had cut Andrew Pengilly to the core, you would have found him white clear through. He was a type of clergyman favored in pious fiction, yet he actually did exist" (p. 240). This is a bad beginning for a characterization, and nothing that follows improves it: the author of a work of fiction has told us that a character he is creating in fiction is as unbelievable as those of fiction—yet does exist (in what sense and where now?). The truth is that in *Elmer Gantry,* in which almost no minister is very good or possesses much religious conviction, the author is overextending himself in the effort to create a good and religious man. He does not want us to mistake this portrait for satire. About all he is able to imagine for a religious man is an unbelievable stereotype which he now wants us to accept as real. Thus from the outset, we suspect that Pengilly will be not a flesh and blood figure but a paper doll. "Mr. Pengilly was a frail stooped veteran with silver hair, thin silver mustache, and a slow smile which embraced the world." He is given a fabulous background. He was a drummer-boy in the Civil War, was clerk in a store, taught Sunday School, was converted by the Indian evangelist Osage Joe, married a passionate girl who died in childbirth, and is ever true to her. He believes his Bible word for word at the same time that he is a mystic. He is a Methodist who keeps Catholic art in his living room. The symbol of his Christian spirit (as well as an example of Lewis's conviction that animals display the unexpected, too) is the fact that "all over the room were the aged dog and ancient cat, who detested each other, never ceased growling at each other, and at night slept curled together" (p. 242).

Pengilly has a powerful spiritual effect upon Frank Shallard, an important figure in the novel who represents a rational, humanitarian, and principled foil to Elmer. Lewis tells us that Frank "began to call his mentor Father Pengilly, and the old man chided him only a little." Soon it is not only Frank who addresses him thus, but the voice of the author also: "For all his innocence and his mysticism,

Father Pengilly was not a fool nor weak." And "he had humor, as well, Father Pengilly." Swept up by Pengilly's power, Lewis goes on: "Not in his garden only but in the woods, along the river, Father Pengilly found God in Nature. He was insane about fishing—though indifferent to the catching of any actual fish. . . . When Father Pengilly mocked him, 'And you have to go books to find God, young man!' then Frank was content to follow him, to be his fellow preacher" (p. 244). In his constant ascription of the word Father to this Methodist preacher, as in Arrowsmith's prayer to God to be free of God, Lewis is utilizing the atheist's presumption to do what he will with religious materials. Somehow sensing the validity of the religious spirit, yet believing in none of the religious practices, Lewis makes fast and loose with any reference or ceremony he chooses. He feels at liberty to mix up all the religious symbols—Jews and Methodists keep crucifixes, for instance. But he does not do it entirely out of mockery; I sense that he yearns to validate religious emotion by converting it to a pantheism that is freed of form so that ceremonies and symbols can become somehow interchangeable.

Spinning fanciful yarns was obsessive, yarns so fanciful that they would have to be brought under control if they were going to be even credible fictions. Such yarn-spinning had dazzled listeners when he was young. But it also irritated realists and anti-romantics, and it alienated him from them. He was still at it in his later years. For instance, he told an interviewer, Betty Stevens, about his plot for a labor play (which must have been some variation on his project for the labor novel that he planned several times and never wrote):

> There's this young radical whippersnapper of a labor organizer. . . . The owner's daughter is working in the factory for the summer, and she falls in love with the organizer. So they try to get the workers to join the union, but the workers won't vote for it. But the owner is a real American, a Dodsworth type of businessman who really believes in unions. So, in the third act, he gets up and makes a speech, telling the workers to join the union. And they do.[22]

This is not great storytelling. It indicates the direction his free-associating mind would take, and it suggests how much more care and discipline would be necessary in the plotting of his best novels.

Fancy, then, required discipline. It could be a source of amusement in his work, yet it could also be the cause of our dismay. We should, though, remember that Lewis countered his fanciful impulses with realistic portraiture. To bring fancy under control he relied upon research, notebooks, and the counsel of experts. For each book Lewis made maps and plans of houses, roads, district, city, state. For *Main Street* he visited small towns. For *Babbitt* he made an exhaustive history of the imaginary city of Zenith, a study of the real estate business, and fact-finding trips to middle-sized cities.[23] Later Lewis engaged Paul de Kruif to give him expertise about the medical profession for use in *Arrowsmith,* and in Kansas City he set up a seminar of preachers to school him in the religious background of *Elmer Gantry.*

Thus there are many figures in Lewis who are not the result of the working of enchantment. Vida Sherwin of *Main Street* is one of these. She is a schoolteacher whom Lewis describes as "small and active and sallow" (p. 250). "She lived an engrossed useful life," he says, "and seemed as cool and simple as an apple. But secretly she was creeping among fears, longing, and guilt." Before his marriage, Dr. Kennicott teases Vida at a card party and on a sleigh-ride, and though he quickly forgets her, she yearns for him, amidst confusing emotions, which she fights out in prayer; no one knows of her "abyss of passion." She is equally confused in her attitude toward Carol, who becomes "a part of her" because of their shared love, yet is an object of jealousy. Then Vida flirts with and encourages Raymie Wutherspoon, and they are married. She becomes more plump, less "admiring of marital bliss," less sentimental, more strident. This brief portrait uncovers a hidden life and seems to take its example from Masters or Anderson. It is skillfully done.

Though flamboyance and humor were his modes, Lewis could occasionally strike a character of quiet realism. Paul Riesling and Seneca Doane of *Babbitt* and Edith Cortright of *Dodsworth* are further examples. But Perry Miller observed that Lewis was basically "in love with mythological and typological creations like Micawber and Gradgrind, and all his effort had been to evoke such genii out of the American bottle."[24] Lewis's range was large, however, and he could sketch characters from both fancy and observation. What makes his attitudes complex, though, is that he pursued enchantments given to him by romantic fiction—and he did so all his life really—yet he followed trends in realism also and came to dislike many of the preconceptions he discovered in himself and others and attacked these preconceptions vigorously.

Chapter 5

The Apprentice Fiction

Our Mr. Wrenn, Lewis's first novel, opens with a quixotic fantasy. William Wrenn, 34, a "little man" like many of Wells's characters, nods to the brass-buttoned ticket-taker in front of the Nickelorion Moving-Picture Show and then settles down to watch a travel picture about Java, the destination of his Great Journey, his "heroic roaming," where he will "saunter among dusky Javan natives" in markets and temples. Such films as this, rather than print (except for Kipling's "Mandalay thing") feed his imagination, and in the course of the novel Wrenn believes himself to be a knight, adventuring in exotic lands, courting a beloved lady, defying enchanted foes, and transforming reality into dreams. He expresses his quixotic yearnings to a horse, his momentary Rosinante standing at a street-corner: "Poor old fella. What you thinking about? Want to be a circus horse and wander? Le's beat it together. You can't, eh? Poor old fella!"[1]

William Wrenn has a tedious job and a lonely life in New York; he inhabits a milieu of office, luncheonette, boarding house, and movie palace. Timid and lonely, he yearns for excitement, particularly the excitement of travel. "Everywhere the world, to his certain witnessing, was turned to crusading, to setting forth in great ships as if it were again in the brisk morning of history when the joy of adventure possessed the Argonauts." To Chicago, Washington, the South, "thither the iron horses would be galloping, their swarthy smoke manes whipped back by the whirlwind. . . . In time he also would mount upon the iron coursers and charge upon Chicago . . ." (pp. 9–10).

Emboldened by an unexpected legacy of nearly a thousand dollars, he quits his dull job as a clerk and signs onto a cattleboat (even as Lewis himself had done). Aboard ship he finds within himself a latent source of courage and wins a fight with a drunken bully. His courage soon falls away, however, as England, seen under the guidance of a bohemian artist named Istra Nash, confuses and defeats him. He becomes, as Lewis said in a comment on the book, "as retchingly homesick as I had been on just the same sort of trip after Freshman year in college"; Wrenn, Lewis goes on, "wisely returned to clerkship and littleness."[2]

The transmuting power of the quixotic imagination is at work in Wrenn. When he first sees Istra Nash in London, he thinks her "a freak," but, turning loose his fantasies, he instantly "made up a whole novel about her. Gee! She was a French countess, who lived in a reg'lar château, and she was staying in Bloomsbury incognito, seeing the sights" (p. 84). He imagines that she has stolen the family gold and has come to England to study medicine. Istra tries to shut off these fantasies by telling Wrenn that she is simply an American studying art in Paris. But to no avail.

Istra is a pseudo-artist, of little accomplishment, who plays at life and creates nothing. For her, "play" is the free spirit's answer to inhibitions. She promises to teach Wrenn how to play. But Wrenn has his own skill as a fantasist. When he hears Istra sobbing in the next room, he imagines saying to her, "Please let me help you, princess, jus' like I was a knight" (p. 91). Medieval fancy grips his mind. Somehow, after he returns to New York, Wrenn must break that grip and find reality instead. He rebels against Istra and discovers Nellie Croubel, whom he can marry.

At the end, Wrenn muses upon his changed character, especially his loss of illusions. Looking across the East River, he "mourns," "Gee! . . . it's the first time I've noticed a sunset for a month! I used to see knights' flags and Mandalay and all sorts of stuff in sunsets!" The novel concludes with his plan to spend the evening playing cards with his wife, the modest and practical Nellie, and reading the paper aloud. He is heard chuckling "softly to himself as he hurried home through the brisk autumn breeze with seven cents' worth of potato salad" (p. 254). The novel is a trifle, but in it Lewis has made a step toward establishing the model of a quixote and the pattern of the conflicts of his fiction.

In Lewis's second novel, *The Trail of the Hawk*, "Carl Ericson (some day to be known as 'Hawk' Ericson) [is] the divinely restless seeker of the romance that must—or we die!—lie beyond the hills" (p. 5). Men from the East having expended themselves, westerners possess the future. It was for Carl "to carry on the American destiny of extending the Western horizon; his to restore the wintry Pilgrim virtues and the exuberant, October, partridge-drumming days of Daniel Boone; then to add, in his own or another generation, new American aspirations for beauty" (p. 6). In the same spirit, Lewis wrote the following dedication to Carl's future: "He saw the vision of the America through which he might follow the trail like the pioneers whose spiritual descendent he was" (p. 121). Ericson envisions the noble panorama that tempts the vagabond:

> Cities of tall towers; tawny deserts of the Southwest and the flawless sky of cornflower blue over sage-brush and painted butte; silent forests of the Northwest; golden China dragons of San Francisco; old orchards of New England; the oily Gulf of Mexico where tramp steamers puff down to Rio; a snow-piled cabin among somber pines of northern mountains. Elsewhere, elsewhere, elsewhere, beyond the sky-line, under larger stars, where men ride jesting and women smile. (p. 122).

We find a mixture of images from pioneering and medieval romance. Writing of Carl's departure from home by train, Lewis adds images from ancient mythology to images of pioneers and medieval knights: "None of the sleepy passengers saw that the Golden Fleece was draped about him or that under his arm he bore the harp of Ulysses" (p. 124). The destiny, the vision, the wanderlust of the pioneers, knights, and ancient heroes—all were imagined to exist in the Midwest, to whose landscape Carl makes a dreamy response and from whose western winds he draws strength.

Bone Stillman, the socialist pariah who is Carl's mentor, has given the boy advice about life: First, says Stillman, don't live calf-bound in books: live in life. Second, be wary of refining influences and of imitations. Third, have a big ambition: "You want to keep on remembering that Chicago's beyond Joralemon, and Paris beyond Chicago, and beyond Paris—well, maybe there's some big peak of the Himalayas" (p. 50). And fourth, beware that love and marriage don't take away your freedom.

For knights such as Carl, women are both an inspiration and a temptation. In fact, before winning his princess, Carl not only is almost distracted from his purposes by a simple home-body named Gertie, but is almost seduced by a wicked tentshow performer; luckily, he escapes both. He spends a short time at Plato College, where Professor Frazer introduces him to a wide range of romantic poets—Shelley, Keats, Whitman, Swinburne, and Rossetti. Frazer's lectures explain Shaw and Wells: "These men have perceived that this world is . . . a collection of human beings completely related . . . so that if we would take thought all together, and work together, as a football team does, we would start making a perfect world" (p. 81). The sports metaphor indicates the quixotic inspiration of Frazer's dream. Furthermore, Frazer spins a socialist fantasy: "the defeat of death; the life period advancing to ten-score years all crowded with happy activity. The solution of labor's problem; . . . a way out for the unhappy consumer. . . . A real democracy and the love of work that shall come when work is . . . joyously shared in a community inclusive of the living beings of all nations" (p. 82). But Frazer is run out of town by reactionary faculty and villagers. And Carl leaves, too.

Carl's career follows the quixotic quest. He wanders up and down the land, learning and searching. In California he becomes master of "the fastest steeds that ever had been known"—airplanes. Soon he is in the lists—as a racing pilot. The realistic portrayal of airplanes and air shows makes the middle section of the book (called "The Adventure of Adventure") its most convincing part. An injury to Carl and the deaths of several pilot-friends cause him to quit racing and turn to business. What follows after his arrival in New York, however, is pure romance.

"The Adventure of Love" is the title of Part III of the novel. We are now fully exposed to Lewis's concept of "play," which he had introduced briefly through Istra Nash in *Our Mr. Wrenn.* Play expresses Lewis's romantic, as opposed to his satiric, view of life. It is what most of his women and many of his men yearn for. It is their answer to oppressive reality. Play means games, make-believe, fantasy, and escape into nature. It nourishes the flagging spirit. The dreams are lost, childhood has flown, but the yearning remains, and an unhappy man or woman, knowing no way to recover, feels an upsurging hope in the discovery of a playfellow; they will be "kids," or brother and sister, to each other.

Playmate Ruth Winslow enters *The Trail of the Hawk* with the kind of description one expects in *True Romances:* "Ruth was twenty-four, perhaps, or twenty-five. Not tall, slight enough to nestle, but strong and self-reliant. She had quantities of dark-brown hair, crisp and glinty, though not sleek. . . . Her smile was made irresistible by her splendidly shining teeth. . . . She was young and clean, sweet without being sprinkled with pink sugar" (pp. 254–55). To understand the importance and impact of play, we should recall that Carl, known as "the Hawk," had been a daring racing pilot and

(Lewis said later) an anticipation of Lindbergh. Yet the language of the book undermines Carl's heroism. To his "blessed" Ruth, for instance, Carl puts the choice between being a New Woman and a soft, weak creature as follows: "Would you rather be a perfect lady and have blue bowls with bunnies on them for your very worst dissipation, or be like your mountain-climbing woman and have anarchists for friends one day and be off hiking through the clouds the next?" (p. 286). "So," writes Lewis, "they talked, boy and girl, wondering together what the world really is like" (p. 287). It is hard to believe that much understanding of the world can come of such a mixture of fancy and incoherence.

One time a hike takes the lovers to a friend's home, where, alone and playing at marriage, they are confronted by the realities of sexual attraction. Lewis naïvely discloses to his reader that sexuality is a genuine force within men; this timid insight was as much as he had absorbed of the changing attitudes that Dreiser and other naturalists were exploring. "Carl did some swift thinking. He was not above flirting. . . . There was a feeling of sudden intimacy which might mean anything. Only . . . she had been so quiet, so frank, so evidently free from a shamefaced erotic curiosity, that now he instantly dismissed the query, 'How far could I go? What does she expect?' which, outside of pure-minded romances, really does come to men" (pp. 293–94).

Then Lewis continues: "It was a wonderful relief to dismiss the query; a simplification to live in the joy each moment gave of itself. The hour was like a poem. Yet he was no extraordinary person; he had, in the lonely hours of a dead room, been tortured with the unmoral longings which, good or bad, men do feel" (p. 294). Still under the influence of chivalry, yet touched by new currents of thought, Lewis was not prepared to break with the demands of commercial readership.

From this point on, the word "play" or some form of it occurs frequently. Page 322 is typical. Carl pleads with Ruth not to marry his rival: "You'll play with me awhile, won't you?" Again, he cries, "You will let me be your playmate, even as much as Phil is, while we're still—." And she answers, "Carl, I've never played as much with anyone as with you."

Excerpts from Ruth's fantasies further illustrate this kind of romance: "I'm the Spirit of Spring. . . I'm a poet. I've thought it all out and decided that I shall be the American Sappho. . . . You're to buy me a book and take me down to the Maison Epinay for tea, and read me poetry while I yearn over the window-boxes and try to look like a Nicollette. Buy me a book with spring in it, and a princess, and a sky like this—corn-flower blue with bunny-rabbit clouds" (p. 334). When she sees an old man in the park, she dares Carl to say to him, "I prithee, sir, of thy good will come thou forthfaring with two vagabonds who do quest high and low the land of Nowhere" (p. 335).

The ending of *The Trail of the Hawk* is poorly resolved. Neither here, nor in *The Job* nor in *Main Street,* did Lewis reveal much skill in terminating his early novels. After Ruth and Carl Ericson wed, we hurriedly and sketchily follow the first few months of their marriage. Lewis is uncertain what should come next. One obvious possibility (if there really was any need to take the novel beyond the wedding) was to give the Ericsons a home, a community, a job, and a family. But romance prefers escape and far-off places. Hawk and his wife leave for South America. Ericson's philosophy is expressed in the novel's last sentence: "How bully it is to be living, if you don't have to give up living in order to make a living" (p. 409), a childish echo of a Wellsian idea that modern industrial and commercial society stifles the spirit. The deadly office routine is especially singled out here (as it is in *The Job* and in the short stories) for its ability to bring the spirit down. One's work must be exciting or one must be doomed to a life of aching yearning. To combat the disillusionment, to destroy the boredom—these are the purposes of play, so that life will be ever innocent and hopeful.

Medieval romance sets the tone of dozens of Lewis's short stories. I will choose only a few examples. Young Lewis had filled his notebooks with his impressions, his observations, and his ideas for plot and theme. Though he had written stories during his college days and during his sojourn in California, he all but abandoned the form while working as an editor in New York City and seeing through to publication several of his novels. The bibliography in Schorer's life of Lewis lists only seven short stories from 1910 to 1915 (pp. 815–19). In 1915, however, Lewis began five years of prodigious output of the magazine story, which became for him an easy source of income. Grace Lewis remembered that after *The Trail of the Hawk* was finished she asked her husband why he did not start writing short stories again as a change. Lewis replied that he didn't think he had the short story mind, "that he needed more room to turn round."

Mrs. Lewis urged him to look at his notebooks, and within a week, she recalled, he had written "Nature, Incorporated," for which he was paid five hundred dollars. Mrs. Lewis went on: "He was simmering with ideas. If he only wrote one story a month that would be six thousand [dollars] a year."[3] From 1915 to 1919 the newly-married couple wandered about the nation, while Lewis worked on short stories and novels, did research for *Main Street,* and finally pushed that book through to completion, all on money earned from the sale of magazine fiction.

By and large, the quality of Lewis's short stories is not high. Out of some seventy Lewis stories, most anthologists have found only one ("Young Man Axelbrod") worth reprinting. We should remember, however, that Lewis was aware of the compromises of magazine writing: after *Main Street* he would pledge: "I don't believe I shall ever again be the facile [Saturday Evening] Post trickster I by God was—."[4] Yet even with this warning against overestimating the quality of his tales, Lewis gave license to examine them seriously, for he wrote of them to Carl Van Doren in 1921: "And even in my magazine stories (yes, even in the serial *Free Air* . . .) I have steadily sought to work out a means of doing as honest work as the powerful negations of the magazine editors would permit. Out of perhaps fifty stories . . . I doubt if more than ten could with the slightest justice be classed as 'brisk and amusing chatter.' "[5]

In "Honesty, If Possible," Terry Ames, an advertising writer for a real estate firm, has come from a small town to the metropolis, where he is confronted by the blankness of life and its unchanging gray days. He is an idealist and altruist, but the city tells him to stick narrowly to his work. A new clerk arrives, beautiful Susan Bratt, whom Terry protects from the crude wolves of the office. Terry and Susan come to recognize that they share a mutual disillusionment and a mutual ideal. They belong, says Terry, to the same race of people, who "aren't content with just galumping along and making a living, but have to fuss round and take all the joy out of life by wanting people to be honest or efficient or original."[6] Their moment of recognition finds characteristic language. Sue says, "Poor tired Terry Ames and Sue Bratt what want to run and play in the meadows!" He responds, "We are just kids, aren't we, dear?" Such dialogue is common in dozens of stories. Clearly, Lewis would have to rid himself of it in order to do major writing.

"The Hidden People" tells how wisdom comes to another midwesterner in New York. Julian Oliver, a clerk, becomes acquainted with Miss Quinn, a manicurist who knows the importance of remaining decent in the big city. She tells Julian that because he, the innocent country boy, does not know about real things, like love and death and poverty, she must introduce him to the "Village of Hidden People"—janitors, elevator operators, manicurists who are friendly and sincere amidst the great, cruel, and impersonal city. It is the little people who have strength and goodness, not the sophisticates, the pretenders, the bohemians, the cultured. Miss Quinn, imparting her strength to Julian, plans his life for him and promises to marry him when they are both worthy. "He was hoping to rise from his social class, of smug little talkers, to her class, of the Hidden People who do the world's work and give without ceasing."[7] Although it would be inadvisable to take this shallow and sentimental story too seriously, "The Hidden People" does embody thoughts and emotions which are central to Lewis's fiction as a whole. It reveals a persistent puzzlement about human nature which exists in the dichotomy between the good "little people" and the evil educated sophisticates.

"Young Man Axelbrod," Lewis's most admired short story, contains many of the motifs of knighthood, but substitutes the pathos of age for the silliness of youth. The opening passages reflect Lewis's admiration for the "escape" elements in *Walden;* farmer Axelbrod has retired to a shack in the woods of Minnesota, where he continues his life-long self-education. There, "baching it," he reads "big, thick, dismal volumes of history and economics."[8] As a quixote must, Axelbrod stumbles on some romances of college life, and dreams of the Mount of Muses, of ancient groves, avid learners, and sympathetic instructors. To realize his dreams, he enrolls at Yale at the age of sixty-four. But as a freshman, Knute meets reality instead of idealism—the reality of a hustling roommate, toadying aesthetes, and cynical professors. Dismayed, he finds one friendship which satisfies his yearning spirit. He meets Gilbert Washburn, a fictional counterpart of young Lewis, who "doesn't go out for anything." They recognize what unites them: "We came here to dream." Together these unknown undergraduates attend a concert by Ysaye. Like so much meaningful experience in Lewis, the music brings thoughts of knighthood: "In the music of Ysaye . . . Knute had found all the incredible things of which he had slowly been reading in William Morris and 'Idylls of the King.' Tall knights he had beheld, and slim princesses in white samite, the misty gates of forlorn towns, and the glory of the chivalry that never was." Again, knighthood leads to pioneerdom, for after the concert Washburn lures Knute into tales of the pioneer days. Thus they were "wandering minstrels," Gilbert the troubadour with his man-at-arms. After exploring the ghetto of New Haven and reading some poetry, Knute returns to Minnesota fulfilled, his idealism justified.

Lewis's third novel, *The Job,* is a significant step forward in characterization and social commentary, as well as in the technique of getting them down on paper in ways which can reward our attention today; nonetheless, we see in the novel many of the perennial faults, compromises, and slips in control. *The Job* is a realistic novel, with subordinate passages of both romance and satire. In it Lewis attempted to deal sympathetically with the problems of the New Woman. Under the coaching of his bride ("When Hal was writing it I had dug back into my mind for all my reactions to my own job days," Grace Lewis has said[9]), his protagonist is a serious, talented, and generally admirable young feminist who leaves the small town in order to seek self-development in New York City. At first glance, Una Golden (whose name is Spenserian and within the orbit of medievalism) might appear to be another of Lewis's small town romantics; the novel opens in Panama, Pennsylvania, and Una, at twenty-four, is "as glowing as any princess of balladry." She has been waiting for the fairy prince, yearning for someone to love. But the author assures us that Una is a "matter-of-fact idealist" (p. 5)—that is, she somehow tempers "idealism" with "reality." Facing up to her discontentments, to her lack of opportunities, and to the dullness of village life, she determines to go adventuring in New York. Without knowing that there was such a program as feminism, she had become a feminist, "demanding the world" (p. 25).

In New York she attends secretarial school. Her first job (and this novel is the record of a succession of jobs) is difficult and dull, full of petty decisions. For a moment, however, Walter Babson, Una's prince, appears. He courts Una, and Lewis presents several scenes of sentimental love much in the style of *The Trail of the Hawk.* Lewis could not find language that is simple in structure yet expressive of deep feeling. He is caught, not only in the literary language of the genteel tradition, but in the cheap language of the popular magazines. So Walter says, "Poor kids . . . trying to be good slaves in an office when we want to smash things" (p. 77); "civilization . . . tells us to work like fiends all day and be lonely and respectable all evening" (p. 104). At the point of involvement, Walter proves no different from Lewis's other boyish heroes; he simply excuses himself and leaves for Omaha. Una is shocked back to reality once more, and she continues her education by trial and disillusionment.

Her life becomes entwined with that of Eddie Schwirtz, whose entrance marks an important stage in Lewis's writing career. Eddie is Lewis's first full realization of the babbitt-type. Furthermore, Lewis mixes and balances diverse qualities in Una's character in order to convince us that she could make the error of marrying Eddie. Una possesses both credulousness and disillusionment, pliability and strength, optimism and despair. Thus she is bemused into thinking Schwirtz direct, kindly, and jolly, like hometown people. After all, Una, though a seeker after education and enlightenment in the metropolis, retains much of her provincial background (she is not above reciting "I'm Only Mammy's Pickanniny Coon" for Eddie). In Schwirtz, too, Lewis combines affability with a momentary softness and loneliness, as Eddie's desire for Una holds his vulgarity in check.

The crisis comes when Una, desperately tired from overwork, sees marriage—any marriage—as the escape from loneliness. Schwirtz is the only man available to her, and she marries him. At once she learns of his true nature. She "dreaded always the memory of that first cataclysmic night of their marriage; and mourned [it], as in secret, for year on year, thousands of women do mourn" (p. 246). When sometime later Eddie reports that he has a venereal disease, Una leaves him. Her marriage, however, has been an experience in which she has comprehended moral weakness. She now begins a successful career as a real estate saleswoman, and at the age of thirty-four, like an advanced feminist, she thinks of adopting a child. Instead she becomes the manager of a chain of hotels, finding the work that she is good at and that "needs her." The book ends abruptly. By a startling coincidence, the publicity man of the hotel firm is Walter Babson, still unmarried. Perhaps Lewis and his publishers could not as yet admit that Una's experience would lead her to new encounters. At any rate only the most sentimental of readers could be pleased with the book's ending. Una will get a divorce. Walter expresses their dreams of marriage: they will have a bungalow, a Ford, two cats, a library of Wells and Compton Mackenzie and Anatole France. The novel reverts to the language of play. They will be, Walter says, "two lonely kids that curl up close" (p. 326).

The story of Milt Daggett in *Free Air* is that of another pioneer-knight.[10] In Milt the adventurous spirit is combined with the ingenuity and creativity of the natural mechanic. The path of Claire Boltwood, an eastern princess, crosses his, and Milt at once abandons his car-repair shop and follows her westward. Throughout the novel, Claire gets into scrapes, and Milt, riding his humble steed (a little car) arrives in time to save her, protect her, and awkwardly woo her.

An innocent exuberance impels the novel. *Free Air* is a hymn to the West—every westward mile teaches and regenerates. Milt aspires to enroll in a Seattle college and study engineering; Claire's ill father regains his health on the trip; and Claire herself learns the important western values of life, which the East cannot teach and which she soon recognizes in Milt and sees lacking in her fiancé, Jeff Saxton of New York, who is effete, overmannered, and snobbish.

Milt is sufficiently entranced by lost knighthood to name his pet cat Lady Vere de Vere. While she is his only companion, he often talks to her. Western splendor animates Milt to a realization of the possible beauty of poetry and the glory of words. Suddenly, Milt makes an important utterance. He expresses a thought which might well supply the theme for most of Lewis's novels (note especially *Dodsworth*): Milt says, "Wonder if a fellow could be a big engineer, you know, build bridges and so on, and still talk about, oh, beautiful things?" In his halting way, Milt is announcing one of Lewis's central questions: might not the practical man of action—the pioneer who hacks out a civilization or the industrialist who causes it to flourish—devote himself to beauty and art as well as to building?

There is an obvious connection between the pioneer-knights of the early books and the protagonists of subsequent ones, just as there is a connection between the young playing princesses and the later portraits of women. Arrowsmith, Dodsworth, and Timberlane will inherit some of the qualities of Carl Ericson and Milt Daggett. They are western men; they are seekers; they are inventive, curious, adventurous, and chivalrous. That is not to say that they are not quite different also. The younger heroes live lives of shallow experience, no intellectuality, and childlike sensibility. The later protagonists are somewhat older and in many ways more developed. Arrowsmith possesses genius in medical research, Dodsworth struggles with a deep discontent which Ericson and Daggett barely suspect, and Cass Timberlane has resources of stability which come from his dedication to what Lewis called "the quiet mind." Still, they all share both a boyish idealism and, in their relationships with women at least, a continuing naïveté, as if they have not learned—cannot learn—anything about them. In the romantic fiction, furthermore, the younger people yearn hopefully for a richer life, but as innocents whom experience either disillusions or leaves untouched, they succumb to nostalgia or they dumbly push on into the future, as naïve as before.

By means of the context of play which I have presented here, one can come to a better understanding of those female quixotes of his best fiction—Carol Kennicott, Fran Dodsworth, and Jinny Timberlane. One can detect Lewis's fluctuating attitude toward play, from approval to dislike. Knowing, for example, that play was characteristic of Lewis's own courtship of Grace Livingstone Hegger, we can understand better why he ascribed it to the earlier fictional creations he approved of. By the mid-twenties he was estranged from his wife. So we can measure the change in Lewis's evaluation of play by the fact that in *Arrowsmith,* for instance, a much disapproved-of character, Joyce Lanyon, believes in play and tries to use its attractions to divert the hero from accomplishing his important research: in the climactic scene in which he declares his independence of modern America's materialistic temptations, Arrowsmith shouts at Joyce, "You want a playmate and I want to work" (p. 446). Lewis's vision of women had undergone a change.

What an examination of Lewis's apprentice fiction reveals, I think, is the immersion of his early heroes and heroines in the materials of popular fiction, as the quixotic formula requires. It also shows, however, that Lewis himself was entranced by such materials, even though he could often break through to a cautious mockery of them. But as he comes to see that play, bohemianism, vagabondage, and medievalism, for example, are inadequate to a vision of life, he subjects them more decisively to parody. Nonetheless, they linger as the substance of his youth, and they never entirely depart from his work.

Chapter 6

Main Street

Sinclair Lewis's attitude toward the activity of writing can be seen in his letters to his publisher reporting his progress with *Main Street*. The letters overflow with excitement, even though the making of an important novel was for him then, as always, a job as wearing as the most strenuous manual labor. "Whether it's good or not," he wrote, "of course I can't tell, but there is this fact usually indicative of some excellence: I'm enormously enjoying writing it . . . indeed I'm not thinking of much else."[1] He *was* thinking of other matters, however; as a former writer of commercial fiction and as a former employee of a publisher's promotion department, he could not help but concern himself with sales. He gave some thought to marketing his short stories and to advertising his recent novel *Free Air*. He was involved in all the activities of his profession.

He sensed, according to these letters, what *Main Street* might mean to him: ". . . all my thoughts and planning are centered in *Main Street*—which may, perhaps, be the real beginning of my career as a writer."[2] And later: "I believe that it will be the real beginning of my writing. No book and no number of short stories I've ever done have ever meant a quarter of what this does to me."[3] In the spring of 1920 he wrote that the pace was exhausting, but his excitement was unabated: "Yesterday . . . was the first day I'd taken off in eleven days; even last Sunday I worked till 5:30 P.M. I'm revising with the most minute care and, I fancy, with success."[4]

Then at the end of July he completed the book. He had managed to finish it, Lewis said, "only by working eight hours a day, seven days in most weeks, though a normal number of daily hours of creative writing is supposed to be about four. . . . [sic] I never worked so hard, and never shall work so hard, again . . . unless Comes the Revolution and I am driven from writing to real work, like bricklaying or soldiering or being a nursemaid."[5] He thus concludes with characteristic irony, belittling enough and repeated often enough so that one may wonder what his reservations about writing were. He spoke of writing as "sweaty and nerve-jangling," and said that pure research in a laboratory would have pleased him more.[6] To some extent such yearning is one of Lewis's poses. Yet a study of his books does show that he chose research in the laboratory as a metaphor for the life best lived, though he also commended the careers of the physician, the inn-keeper, and the architect. For instance, "I never quite get over the feeling," Lewis told an interviewer in 1947, "that writing isn't much of a profession, compared with being a doctor, that it's not quite manly to be sitting there on the seat of your pants all the time."[7] Professor Perry Miller remembered a conversation following an outburst of temper when Lewis discovered that his brother Claude would not attend one of the novelist's lectures during their tour of Europe. Miller writes that Lewis cried out: "It's been that way from the beginning. . . . I wanted to write, and I've worked like hell at it, and the whole of Sauk Centre and my family and America have never understood that it is work, that I haven't just been playing around, that this is every bit as serious a proposition as Claude's hospital. When you said that Claude did not want to hear my lecture . . . you set up all the resentments I have had ever since I can remember."[8] Even after he returned to Sauk Centre in 1916 as a successful young author of two novels and a number of stories that had appeared in the *Saturday Evening Post,* the townspeople let him know they considered writing as only "nearly" as choice a trade as medicine, law, the ministry, or even manufacturing.[9] Against these feelings, which he would have throughout his life, Lewis set to work—to hard work—composing *Main Street.*

In his studies of the influence of Cervantes on European and American literature, Professor Harry Levin mentions the resemblance Carol Kennicott bears to Emma Bovary, who is the archetype of the "female quixote."[10] But neither Carol nor *Main Street* has been analyzed thoroughly as an expression of quixotism, though such an analysis can uncover sources of the novel's vitality and appeal.[11] An approach through quixotism can bring us to a better understanding of Carol's ambitions, illusions, conflicts, persistence, and defeat. When seen as the story of a woman with a mind shaped by romantic notions, who challenges the community with her impractical idealism and suffers rebuffs and self-doubt, *Main Street* appears to have more purpose, unity, and psychological interest than many readers have been willing to concede to it.

The quixote's career begins in the library. Of Emma Bovary, Professor Levin writes: "From the drab milieu she has known as a farmer's daughter, her extracurricular reading conjures up the allurements of escape: steeds and guitars, balconies and fountains, medieval and Oriental vistas."[12] We may say much the same thing about Carol, for she can conjure up a bower of roses, a château, a Chinese entertainment, an exotic Frenchman, a poet-lover. She brings to Gopher Prairie a romantic model of what a village should be and a fantasy of her role in life. However, as she settles into her plain and frigid Gopher Prairie home, so different from the one she has imagined, she cries, "How these stories lie!"

The opening chapters of *Main Street* give only fragmentary information about Carol's childhood, but they suggest an environment that encouraged romanticizing. She recalls that her father was "the tenderest man in the world." He created "Christmas fantasies" from "the sacred old rag doll at the tops of the tree," and he would transform the terrors of the night into a "hearth-mythology" of "beneficent and bright-eyed creatures." There were the "tam htab, who is woolly and blue and lives in the bathroom" and "the ferruginous oil stove, who purrs and knows stories." Her father let her read anything she wished, and she is said to have "absorbed" Balzac, Rabelais, Thoreau, and Max Müller at an early age. But what Carol saw in Thoreau, one suspects, was woodsy escapism and inaction, for at one point she recalls, "I used to sit there on the cliffs above Mankato for hours at a time, my chin in my hand, looking way down the valley, wanting to write poems" (pp. 173–74).

At college she announces that she hopes to "conquer the world." Vaporous images from her further reading point to the reformist mission that she must undertake. "She wanted, just now, to have a cell in a settlement-house, like a nun without the bother of a black robe"; from the cell she will improve "a horde of grateful poor." The icon of her dormitory room is "a miniature of the Dancing Bacchante." Having glanced at a book on town improvement, she plans to convert a village to the greens and garden-walls of France. Or she wishes to "turn a prairie town into Georgian houses and Japanese bungalows." She declares, "I don't understand myself but I want—everything in the world! Maybe I can't sing or write, but I know I can be an influence in library work. Just suppose I encouraged some boy and he became a great artist!" (p. 9).

Meanwhile she is learning to transmute reality. For instance, as she climbs along the banks of the Mississippi, she sees the river as her fanciful mind dictates. She listens to the fables of the river "about the wide land of yellow waters and bleached buffalo bones to the West; the Southern levees and singing darkies and palm trees toward which it was forever mysteriously gliding; and she heard again the startled bells and thick puffing of high-stacked river steamers wrecked on sand-reefs sixty years ago. Along the decks she saw missionaries, gamblers in tall pot hats, and Dakota chiefs with scarlet blankets" (p. 6). She has created a tableau peopled with figures of her own imagining—dreams, Lewis says later, "governed by the fiction she had read, drawn from the pictures she had envied" (p. 234). To give another illustration of her fancy, at the commencement exercises at Blodgett College "she saw the palms as a jungle, the pink-shaded electric globes as an opaline haze, and the eye-glassed faculty as Olympians" (p. 8).

During a year in Chicago after graduation, these impulses are strengthened. Carol spends an evening at a bohemian studio party, where she hears talk of "Freud, Romain Rolland, syndicalism, the Confédération Générale du Travail, feminism vs. haremism, Chinese lyrics, nationalization of mines, Christian Science, and fishing in Ontario" (p. 10). Significantly, her first job is at the library in St. Paul where, while she works, she reads "scores of books." The subject list is especially suited to the development of her fancy: "volumes of anthropology . . . , Parisian imagistes, Hindu recipes for curry, voyages to the Solomon Isles, theosophy with modern American improvements" (p. 10). At dances, "in dread of life's slipping past, she turned into a bacchanal." Her sense of mission returns; she will transform and redesign a prairie town.

At this point, Dr. Will Kennicott enters her life. He woos her by exploiting her desire to find a purpose for herself, declaring that his village needs her. Dr. Kennicott provides a notable occasion for us to apprehend the way in which the vision of the quixote converts reality to illusion. As we noted earlier, he shows Carol some photographs, and, though they are streaked and vague, she perceives them as (in her need for adventure) she must. She sees his amateurish snapshots of lakes as "etchings" that delineate "snow in crevices of a boggy bank, the mound of a muskrat house, reeds in thin black lines." Intuiting Carol's nature, Kennicott uses one picture especially well. It shows a forest clearing and a log cabin. In front of the cabin is "a sagging woman with tight-drawn hair, and a baby bedraggled, smeary, glorious-eyed." Kennicott tempts Carol by saying, "Look at that scared baby! Needs some woman with hands like yours. Waiting for you!" (pp. 18–19). Carol succumbs. Such photographs will return later in the novel, when Kennicott is courting Carol again after her flight from Gopher Prairie. At the middle when she visits the home of this baby in the snapshot, she would tell him of Prince Charming, but he doesn't understand (p. 188).

After Carol and the doctor marry, they ride the train into Gopher Prairie, the town she will "conquer" and reform. She has her first view of the reality she must work with. When she sees their house and her room, the shock is great. She blames her reading. "She glanced at the houses; tried not to see what she saw; gave way in: 'Why do these stories lie so? They always make the bride's homecoming a bower of roses. Complete trust in the noble spouse. Lies about marriage. . . . And this town—O my God! I can't go through with it. This junk-heap!'" (p. 29). She has read "too many books." She goes to the bedroom window "with a purely literary thought of village charm—hollyhocks and lanes and apple-cheeked cottagers." What she sees is "the side of the Seventh-Day Adventist Church—a plain clapboard wall of a sour liver color" (p. 32). *This* was "the terraced garden below her boudoir"—"How these stories lie!" Muttering, "I'm mildly insane," she goes out to see the village, the "empire" she is going to "conquer." She takes that memorable promenade which we have already noted. She finds a Main Street characterized by the reek of blood from the meat market, by yellow buildings, by a cat sleeping on the lettuce in the grocery window. But Carol is not broken by that view of the village. For a long time she survives and returns to the fray. Her resiliency originates in her transmuting imagination; she is like Don Quixote with bandaged head taking to the road once more. Her enthusiasm, at least at first and in one so young ("plastic" and "innocent," as Lewis says) is even engaging.

Her adventures test not only Carol's notions but also the beliefs and actions of society. In the face of the challenge that she brings, members of the community reveal themselves as corrupt and hypocritical—or at least foolish in their own way. For instance, when Carol attends her first party in Gopher Prairie, she carries to it the image of herself as "a smart young married woman in a drawing room, fencing with clever men." She expects good talk, and she believes that she can enter into conversation as an equal to the men. But they have been arguing all evening about the kind of dog an old-timer had owned years ago. When Carol confronts them with a question about labor relations, she draws from them remarks that are the hallmark of Lewis's satire. Jackson Elder asserts that he is for freedom and constitutional rights: "If any man don't like my shop, he can get up and git. Same way, if I don't like him, he gits. And that's all there is to it." He mumbles on about such "poppycock" as profit-sharing, welfare work, insurance, old-age pensions. It "enfeebles a workman's independence—and wastes a lot of honest profit" (pp. 49–50).

By such a pattern of challenge and reaction throughout the novel, each satiric monologue achieves its organic place. At every thrust from Carol, a villager exposes his own foolishness or hypocrisy about education, economics, politics, religion. Each encounter provides Lewis with the opportunity to exhibit his virtuosity in creating the grotesque rantings of gossips, churchwomen, preachers, journalists, and boosters. Carol induces the community to expose itself. Her own response to these encounters remains unchanging, nonetheless. Even as she drags herself homeward from them, past a "hulking house," "a streaky yellow pool," a "morass," she tells herself that "her beautiful town" still exists—in her mind (p. 139). She believes in the village she has imagined. What she is now seeking is a person to share it with.

Several secondary figures in *Main Street* reinforce Carol's quixotism. Guy Pollock, whom Lewis declared to have been the protagonist of the book in its earliest conception (though no draft of that version exists and Lewis's biographer doubts whether such a version ever got on paper[13])—Pollock too is maddened by reading. He "hints his love" for Sir Thomas Browne, Thoreau, Agnes Reppelier, Arthur Symons, Claude Washburne, and Charles Flandrau, authors who can nourish the fancy. Carol visits Pollock at his rooms, where he reveals the content of his imagination. Here, he says, are his "office, town-house, and château in Picardy. But you can't see the château and town-house (next to the Duke of Sutherland's)" (p. 154). Of course Carol *can* see them, quite as well as he can. Carol and Pollock discuss the possibility of reforming the town, but Pollock is by now incapable of rebellion. Like Prufrock, he wishes only to be an attendant, "the confidant of the old French plays, the tiring-maid with the mirror and the loyal ears" (p. 159). Carol wonders whether Pollock might be her Prince Charming, but she later realizes that he was only a frame on which she hung "shining garments."

Toward her husband, Carol feels a genuinely painful conflict. Kennicott is a capable doctor, but his very competence is paradoxically a problem for Carol, who finds that capable people are often shallow and bigoted. At their best, without what Lewis would two years later call "babbittry," these figures are heroes, "doers," for whom "all this romance stuff is simply moonshine." Kennicott shows admirable courage and ability as a physician and surgeon in several crises. But even at such moments Carol must recreate him in romanticized and literary terms: she "saw the drama of his riding by night to the frightened household on the distant farm; pictured children standing at a window, waiting for him. He suddenly had in her eyes the heroism of a wireless operator on a ship in a collision; of an explorer, fever-clawed, deserted by his bearers, but going on–" (p. 177). She tells Pollock that he and she are "a pair of hypercritical loafers, . . . while [Will] quietly goes and does things" (p. 180). She restates the dichotomy: to deal with the farmers Kennicott "speaks a vulgar, common, incorrect German of life and death and birth and the soil," while she reads "the French and German of sentimental lovers and Christmas garlands." Such a division lies at the heart of the book, though Will calls Carol neurotic, and she labels him stupid. But Carol, the doctor, and the novel itself are considerably more complex than this formulation suggests, and Carol knows it upon reflection. This complexity is creditable in ways that have been forgotten by Lewis's detractors. Carol knows that Kennicott is not simply a quiet doer. He is noisy, opinionated, narrow, prejudiced, quarrelsome, and unfaithful, and the novel takes pains to display him as such. Carol's neurosis, meanwhile, is compounded of idealism, enthusiasm, doubt, disillusionment, and alienation.

In the midst of her despair, Carol inquires into books once more in an effort to understand herself and her village. Formerly, in reading popular stories and plays, Carol had found only two traditions about the American town. The first tradition, she reports, "is that the American village remains the one sure abode of friendship, honesty, and clean sweet marriageable girls. . . . The other tradition is that the significant features of all villages are whiskers, iron dogs upon lawns, gold bricks, checkers, jars of gilded cat-tails, and shrewd comic old men who are known as 'hicks' and who ejaculate 'Waal I swan'" (p. 264). Her experience of Gopher Prairie, however, tells her that the town thinks "in cheap motor cars, telephones, ready-made clothes, silos, alfalfa, kodaks, phonographs, leather-upholstered Morris chairs, bridge-prizes, oil-stocks, motion-pictures, land-deals, unread sets of Mark Twain, and a chaste version of national politics." With this small town, Carol—along with hundreds of thousands of young people like her—is not content. She believes that she has derived insight and other "convictions" from her recent reading. She has "driven" her way through books of a somewhat different kind from those she read as a girl. These books were written by the "young American sociologists, young English realists, Russian horrorists; Anatole France, Rolland, Nexo, Wells, Shaw, Key, Edgar Lee Masters, Theodore Dreiser, Sherwood Anderson, Henry Mencken, and all the other subversive philosophers and artists whom women were consulting everywhere" (p. 263).

One night she talks to her friend Vida Sherwin about the dullness, the rigidity, and the sterility of the village. Vida, a "realist," suggests measured steps toward reform. But Carol, for all her new reading and thought, replies that she wants "startling, exotic things": "Strindberg plays, and classic dancers—exquisite legs beneath tulle—and (I can see him so clearly!) a thick, black-bearded, cynical Frenchman who would sit about and drink and sing opera and tell bawdy stories and laugh at our proprieties and quote Rabelais and not be ashamed to kiss my hand!" (p. 270). This is a moment of considerable psychological importance. Whatever the booklist of "American sociologists, French realists, Russian horrorists" may have brought her, Carol's quixotic nature defeats her efforts at new understanding. Her transforming imagination turns Gopher Prairie back into fantasy land.

Romantic love, the motif that particularly directs the yearnings of the female quixote, enters *Main Street* about three-fourths of the way towards its end. When Erik Valborg appears in Gopher Prairie, he is less a substantial character than a projection of what Carol fancies him to be. Much of the confusion surrounding her platonic escapade with Erik occurs because she waivers between at least two images of him. At times she recognizes that he is a commonplace, uneducated, shallow young man; at other times she believes him to be a poet—a Keats or Shelley or (as Lewis plays with Carol's values) an Arthur Upson. Carol is insistent: "He's Keats—sensitive to silken things. . . . Keats, here! A bewildered spirit fallen on Main Street. And Main Street laughs" (p. 339). Thinking of him later, however, she asks herself, "Was he anything but a small-town youth bred on an illiberal farm and in cheap tailor shops?" Valborg himself, like Pollock, brings to his relationship with Carol his own quixotism. It is reported that he reads a great deal, but his taste tends toward "Suppressed Desires" and "The Black Mask." He recalls that, when he lived in Minneapolis, he used to "tramp clear around Lake Harriet, or hike out to the Gates house and imagine it was a château in Italy and I lived in it. I was a marquis and collected tapestries—that was after I was wounded in Padua" (p. 391).

Valborg continues to stimulate and confuse Carol's romantic imagination. While she is doing household tasks, she pictures "herself and a young artist—an Apollo nameless and evasive—building a house in the Berkshires or in Virginia; exuberantly buying a chair with his first check; reading poetry together" (p. 352). She wishes him to be a "playmate," not a lover. She is always dissatisfied, however. In moments of self-awareness, she calls her love affair "pitiful and tawdry. . . . A self-deceived little woman whispering in corners with a pretentious little man" (p. 363). Then she makes a sudden quixotic shift: "No, he is not. He is fine. Aspiring." She is in a turmoil of distraction. She wishes Erik were "a fighter, an artist with bearded surly lips." But "they're only in books." Her mind is spinning, but not toward suicide, like Emma's; Carol knows all too well that the tragedy of her life is "that I shall never know tragedy, never find anything but blustery complications that turn out to be a farce." One moment she is convinced she loves Erik; the next she cannot love him because his wrists are too large, his nose is too snub. She knows that the poem he writes her ("Little and tender and merry and wise / With eyes that meet my eyes") is bad. After Carol and Erik have wandered, talked, and daydreamed for some time, Kennicott confronts her. He is certain he knows what has poisoned her mind: "these fool stories about wives that don't know when they're well off" (p. 363). Her affair ends when Will chases Erik out of town.

About forty pages remain in the novel. Now the problem is whether Carol will retain her illusions or face whatever reality Gopher Prairie presents. She might somehow find a balance of dream and fact that would result in growth. In fact, Levin suggests that the quixotic experience need not end negatively, for it can lead to maturity.[14] But when Carol breaks from Gopher Prairie and settles in Washington, she seems not much different from the person she was before, though she believes herself to be changing. For instance, the "Washington" she finds (or, one suspects, creates) is a city of "leafy parks, spacious avenues, twisty alleys," of "negro shanties turned into studios, with orange curtains and pots of mignonette," of marble houses and butlers and limousines, and "men who looked like fictional explorers and aviators" (p. 426). After a year, her husband comes to woo her back. His gesture is exactly the one he had made when he first courted her about ten years earlier, and her response is just what we expect and fear. "He tossed over to her thirty prints of Gopher Prairie and the country about. . . . She remembered that he had lured her with photographs in courtship days; she made a note of his sameness, his satisfaction with the tactics which had proved good before; but she forgot it in the familiar places" (p. 435). She has built no defense against this well-intuited appeal to her illusions, though she thinks that she has developed what she calls "personal solidarity." Back in Gopher Prairie she wears her eye-glasses on the street (perhaps because she wishes to see more clearly now). The townsmen say of her that "she knows a good deal about books—or fiction anyway," and of her affair with Valborg that it was "just talking books and all that junk." She believes that, though she may not have "fought the good fight," she has kept faith with her ideals.

By seeing Carol Kennicott as a quixote, we come to realize that Lewis could criticize both his heroine and the village. He tried, in his flamboyant, crude, and often careless way, to anatomize a woman torn among illusions and realities. For Carol, Lewis drew upon an archetype, so that Carol touched familiar responses in readers in America, where quixotism has long existed but has not been fully recognized as an important aspect of the national character. In the sub-literature and popular culture of the late nineteenth and early twentieth centuries, romance flourished. We have already noted the cults associated with the Orient, the medieval, the adventurous, the Kiplingesque, poesy, and vagabondia. These formed a state of mind which attracted and repelled several generations of writers. Mark Twain, who understood much of what made and moved America, portrayed quixotism in *Tom Sawyer, Huck Finn, Life on the Mississippi*, and *A Connecticut Yankee.* A towering figure like Mark Twain gathers ideas from the past and opens up potentialities for future writers. His indications of the presence of quixotism in American life are significant; Lewis also sensed such a presence and the conflict that attends it.

Quixotism induces an ambivalent and confusing response, for it embodies both foolishness and idealism. The story of Carol Kennicott is a record of resultant ambiguities. Recognizing that the book is uneven and in some ways inconclusive, we can speculate that the quixotic elements in Lewis's nature disallowed the kind of transcendence that Cervantes and Flaubert achieved. Lewis came to *Main Street* after writing five apprentice novels, among them *The Trail of the Hawk* and *Free Air,* in which young Americans travel the roads in pursuit of adventure and golden ladies. Perhaps he called *Main Street* "the real beginning" of his career because he believed that he was freeing himself from the shackles of romance by satirizing a literary idea of the village that maddens its readers and that had misled him for too long. Carol was his vehicle and victim. Now he was joining a realistic movement that was already well under way without him.

At any rate, I think that we are better informed about *Main Street*—and better able to assess it—if we see it as an account of a quixotic figure—idealistic, disillusioned, of limited vision, yet a challenge to the community. Amidst the comedy, she is, if not tragic, at least worthy of our concern, because her idealism drives her into further suffering. She has been shown that her vision is faulty, weakly inspired, and mistaken, but she continues to see as her aspirations demand. She is more honest and more deceived than anyone around her, and thereby both more trapped and more alive.

Yet Carol continues to seem bewildered in a postscript to the novel, when, later, in an article called "Main Street's Been Paved" written for the *Nation* magazine during the presidential election of 1924, Lewis glanced again at his characters and the condition of their lives. His attitude toward Will Kennicott remained ambivalent. At first, he indicated high praise for the doctor, such praise as he consistently expressed toward the practical "doers" in America: ". . . for him I held, and hold, a Little Brother awe. He is merely a country practitioner, not vastly better than the average; yet he is one of these assured, deep-chested, easy men who are always to be found when you want them, and who are rather amused by persons like myself that go sniffing about, wondering what it all means."[15] This statement seems an echo of Sauk Centre's disapproval of young Harry's "readin' and readin'" in contrast to its admiration for the practical physicians of the Lewis family. It reflects the doubts implanted by the provincial attitude that thought and writing—that art itself—are of no value. Who of the village inquisitors could understand that preparation for the writing career required dreaming and reading and scribbling, and that money and recognition would be slow to appear? One thinks of Lewis's return to Sauk Centre at about thirty-two as an established writer, of his pride in telling the townspeople that he was paid fifteen hundred dollars for a magazine serial which he turned out in two weeks' time; they were awed but not convinced.

Unfortunately, his heroine in *Main Street* falls into the category of small town failures (along with the other impractical dissenters of Gopher Prairie—Miles Bjornstam, Fern Mullins, and Guy Pollock). In "Main Street's Been Paved" Lewis shows us a very beaten "Carol." I have argued that at the end of the novel itself her change or growth was unconvincing. If one considers the *Nation* essay, one doubts even more all Lewis's pretense about her important Washington experience and her personal solidarity. She is hardly recognizable; she appears tired and timid and dumpy; she intends to vote, not for liberal and humanitarian LaFollette, but for Coolidge. Guy Pollock reports that "the doctor has convinced her that to be denunciatory or even very enthusiastic isn't quite respectable." Apparently there was some miscalculation of Carol's "solidarity." But we are not to be left with a simple approval of Kennicott; Lewis, in spite of his awe, is nevertheless aware of Kennicott as a symbol of something dangerous. Lewis lets Guy Pollock, the village lawyer, have the last word. Pollock says, "We've been bullied too long by the Doc Kennicotts and by the beautiful big balloon tires that roll over the new pavement on Main Street—and over our souls." Lewis seems to have shifted to Pollock as spokesman, while meting out to Carol, who will vote for Coolidge, a kind of punishment for the inadequacy of the fanciful notions she, after all, was given by him.

Does *Main Street* pose a choice between Carol's way and Will's way? If he must choose between Carol's qualities as expressed in the novel itself (sensitivity, humanitarianism, curiosity, thoughtfulness, and desire for change and improvement—mixed, however, with impracticality, pretentiousness, artiness, and foolish dreaming) and Will's qualities (practicality, courage, and bluntness—mixed, similarly, with insensitivity, dullness, and scorn for art), which way would Lewis choose? Some critics feel an uncertainty in the novel because of the equivocation between these qualities. Others may feel that the strength of the novel lies in such complexities. Of herself and her husband, Carol theorizes: "There are two races of people, only two, and they live side by side. His calls mine 'neurotic'; mine calls his 'stupid.' We'll never understand each other, never" (p. 294). The tension of the book may be that there is an impossible choice between sensitivity/foolishness and practicality/dullness. But Lewis does shift back and forth in attitude—now praising, now mocking, now admiring, now satirizing. The people of the empire of the Middle West have posed a difficult problem. Lewis continued to ponder the question in subsequent novels until he achieved a resolution in *Dodsworth*. It is sufficient for the moment, though, that in *Main Street* he had taken auspicious steps forward in his attempt to define man, woman, and marriage, and in his continuing search to understand America. Here he had vividly portrayed the provincial locale, commenting upon it in satire which helped open the American mind to new perceptions. He had aroused sleeping consciences to an awareness of hypocrisies and social injustices. He had touched some deeper notes in his portrayal of the heroine—through her loneliness, her misdirected aspirations, and her difficult struggle to find an identity.

Chapter 7

Babbitt

Babbitt, not as much a tale of a quixote as is *Main Street,* nonetheless contains undercurrents of romance, and a reading of the book from the point of view we have been using will reveal some interesting aspects of it.

The book opens with a fantasy. George F. Babbitt, asleep, dreams of a fairy child, an idealized younger sister, imaginary and chaste, "a dream more romantic than scarlet pagodas by a silver sea." Babbitt is not a great reader, as Don Quixote is, but Babbitt's mind is shaped by poetry, by editorials, and by films. For example, in his wallet he kept "clippings of verses by T. Cholmondeley Frink and of the newspaper editorials from which Babbitt got his opinions." Frink can sing songs of vagabondia: "When I am out upon the road, a poet with a pedler's load, I mostly sing a hearty song, and take a chew and hike along, a-handing out my samples fine of Cheero Brand of sweet sunshine . . ." (p. 185). From his newspapers Babbitt gathers information that he garbles: "New York Assembly has passed some bills that ought to completely outlaw the socialists! . . . A mass-meeting in Birmingham's demanded that this Mick agitator, this fellow De Valera, be deported. Dead right, by golly!" (pp. 20–21).

Quixotic romance surrounds Babbitt. The architecture of his Athletic Club, for instance, is pseudo-gothic. "The lobby, with its thick pillars of porous Caen stone, its pointed vaulting, and a brown glazed-tile floor like well-baked bread-crust, is a combination of cathedral-crypt and rathskellar." Further:

> The entrance lobby of the Athletic Club was Gothic, the washroom Roman Imperial, the lounge Spanish Mission, and the reading-room in Chinese Chippendale, but the gem of the club was the dining-room, the masterpiece of Ferdinand Reitman, Zenith's busiest architect. It was lofty and half-timbered, with Tudor leaded casements, an oriel, a somewhat musicianless musician's-

> gallery, and tapestries believed to illustrate the granting of Magna Charta. . . . At one end of the room was a heraldic and hooded stone fireplace which the club's advertising-pamphlet asserted to be not only larger than any of the fireplaces in European castles but of a draught incomparably more scientific (p. 59).

Babbitt's movie theater is the Château, and there he enjoys three kinds of films: "pretty bathing girls with bare legs; policemen or cowboys and an industrious shooting of revolvers; and funny fat men who ate spaghetti" (p. 156). From all these sources, Babbitt derives his romanticism.

Babbitt has his quixotic adventures, too. He wishes he had been a pioneer. His motor car, says Lewis, was "poetry and tragedy, love and heroism." And further: "His office was his pirate ship but the car his perilous excursion ashore." His trips to Maine are his greatest adventures. There he intends to shake loose the family and his wife; there he intends to fish in the male companionship of his friend Paul Riesling and the fishing guides. But such adventures fail him, and shortly after he returns to Zenith you would hardly know he had been away. Another of Babbitt's adventures is to a convention, where he goes out on the town with the boys, and presumably to a prostitute, though nothing very specific is stated.

Babbitt has the power of enchantment, also. As he bathes, he is "lulled to dreaming by the caressing warmth." He is "enchanted" by the dripping water. When he gets into bed, "instantly he [is] in the magic dream," and his fairy child comes to him. In the exhilarations of drinking a cocktail, he feels the urge "to rush places in fast motor cars, to kiss girls, to sing, to be witty." In fancy, he sees himself as a romantic hero, for "the Romantic Hero was no longer the knight, the wandering poet, the cowpuncher, the aviator, nor the brave young district attorney, but the great sales-manager" (p. 143). At the Booster Club, the members designate special titles for the officers and imagine themselves transformed thereby. "It gave to Americans unable to become Geheimräte or Commendatori such unctuous honorifics as High Worthy Recording Scribe and Grand Hoogow."

On his second trip to Maine, "all the way north he pictured the Maine guides: simple and strong and daring, jolly as they played stud-poker in their unceiled shack, wise in woodcraft as they tramped the forest and shot the rapids"—"like a trapper in a Northern Canada movie" (p. 295). But this fancy is dispelled by a truer picture: "In their boarded and rather littered cabin the guides sat about the greasy table playing stud-poker with greasy cards."

But his greatest adventure is his affair with Tanis Judique—and here he exercises his fancy also, transforming her and her friends into persons they are not. His language becomes that of magazine fiction: thinking about what Tanis will wear, Babbitt says, "I can't decide whether you're to put on your swellest evening gown, or let your hair down and put on short skirts and make-believe you're a little girl." He transforms Tanis with these words: "Child, you're the brainiest and the loveliest and finest woman I've ever met! Come now, Lady Wycombe, if you'll take the Duke of Zenith's arm, we will proambulate in to the magnolious feed!" (p. 329). He thinks, "I've dreamed of her all these years and now I've found her!" (p. 332).

Their most memorable excursion "was a tramp on a ringing December afternoon, through snow-drifted meadows down to the icy Chaloosa River. She was exotic in an astrachan cap and a short beaver coat." At the end of the book Babbitt returns to the reality of his wife's appendectomy in order to break these illusions.

Because Babbitt was intended to represent a type, the standardized American citizen to whom he pays homage in his speech before the real estate board, Lewis found himself, while working on the book, puzzling over the problems of typicality and individualization in character-making. Having tried out the babbitt-type, the hustler, the booster, and the charlatan as targets for satire in short stories and several novels, Lewis was by 1921 sensitive to criticism that he was repeating himself. With so many similarities among character, differentiation became a matter of subtle manipulation of details. Lewis's task was to note the differences if he was to individualize effectively. He was aware of the difficulties: "It is true that the Babbitt of Boston, the Babbitt of Charleston and the Babbitt of Seattle are confusingly alike. . . . It is the job of the writer of fiction to discover the differences beneath the similarities."[1] At once, however, Lewis voiced his bitter feeling that in this matter he had been mistreated by unsympathetic critics: "No matter how you differentiate, unless you portray such obviously exceptional, such meretriciously 'quaint' characters as Yankee philosophers or bootleggers, if ever you deal accurately with real contemporaries in Hart, Schaffner & Marx clothes, the critics will accuse you of 'creating nothing but types.' It's a way critics have."

This petulance was as characteristic of Lewis as was his uncertainty about whether he created caricatures or "real" figures. But when his sense of humor overcame his touchiness, Lewis was able to laugh at his struggle in differentiation. To our amusement, in *The*

Man Who Knew Coolidge Lowell Schmaltz talks about the differences among the babbitts of America. The joke comes full circle as Schmaltz directs his scorn toward Lewis himself: "There's a lot of sorehead critics of America that claim we're standardized," but there are, he notes, significant differences. Schmaltz undertakes to show the differences between himself and another Zenith citizen of his acquaintance, a George F. Babbitt by name. Although they both belong to the Athletic Club and to the service clubs, although they have their places of business in the same block and live within a quarter of a mile of each other, although they both like golf and good lively jazz on the radio, yet—

> Well, like this, for instance: I drive a Chrysler, and Babbitt doesn't. I'm a Congregationalist, and Babbitt has no use whatsomever for anything but his old Presbyterian church. He wears these big round spectacles, and you couldn't hire me to wear anything but eyeglasses—much more dignified, *I* think. He's got so he likes golf for its own sake, and I'd rather go fishing, any day. And—and so on. Yes sir, it's a wonderful thing how American civilization, as represented, you might say, by modern advertising, has encouraged the, as a speaker at the Kiwanis recently called it, free play of individualism (p. 48).

Like George F. Babbitt, Lowell Schmaltz evaluates people by tabulating their possessions, and measures individuality by such unimportant and minute distinctions as only such experts in what David Riesman called "marginal differentiation" can perceive. Besides, standardization, in the last analysis, was what Schmaltz and Babbitt most valued, and attention to marginal differences was their empty homage to an older American value of individualism which lingered in their consciences. Yet Lewis made Schmaltz different from Babbitt in ways that Schmaltz cannot see—in Babbitt's discontentment and in his momentary response to the humanitarianism of his friends Paul Riesling and Seneca Doane. Later, in the characterization of Dodsworth, moreover, Lewis moved farther from Schmaltz and from Babbitt. Lewis states that Dodsworth, though he shares some of their attributes, is neither a Schmaltz nor a Babbitt. It is interesting to see how Lewis, serious in *Dodsworth*, as he was not in the passage from *The Man Who Knew Coolidge*, indicates the differences:

> To define what Sam Dodsworth was, at fifty, it is easiest to state what he was not. He was none of the things which most Europeans and many Americans expect in a leader of American industry. He was not a Babbitt, not a Rotarian, not an Elk, not a deacon. He rarely shouted, never slapped people on the back, and he had attended only six baseball games since 1900. He

> knew, and thoroughly, the Babbitts and baseball fans, but only in business.
> While he was bored by free verse and cubism, he thought rather well of Dreiser, Cabell, and so much of Proust as he had rather laboriously mastered. He played golf reasonably well, and did not often talk of his scores. He liked fishing-camps in Ontario, but never made himself believe that he preferred hemlock boughs to a mattress. He was common sense apotheosized (p. 11).

While shouting, back-slapping, and self-conscious masculinity are the primary characteristics of the babbitt-type, Sam Dodsworth has better manners and more sensitivity (though he probably has "mastered" very little art and literature).

Lewis's attention to the matter of types and individuals resulted, I believe, from his desire to be thought of as something more than a satirist. He expressed his feelings in a letter to his editor, in which he said "*all* my keenest eagerest thought tends to sneak off into my plans, thoughts, notes about *Fitch* [an early title for *Babbitt*]—which will, I believe, correct any faults of 'exterior vision,' of sacrifice of personality to types and environment, which in his New Republic review Francis Hackett finds in *Main Street*."[2] In another letter he spoke of George Babbitt as being bigger than Will Kennicott, with "more sensations, more perceptions. . . . He is . . . prosperous but worried, wanting—passionately—to seize something more than motor cars and a house *before it's too late*." Lewis continued, "I want to make Babbitt big in his real-ness, in his relation to all of us, not in the least exceptional, yet dramatic, passionate, struggling."[3] It was carefully planned that Babbitt would have unexpected inner complexities: "where the surprise is going to come in is that, being so standardized, Babbitt yet breaks away from standards, a little, when the time comes."[4] Lewis, hoping to overcome the limitations of caricature, tried consciously to make Babbitt real, yet before the novel was finished, Lewis had conceded something to its inevitable tone and was looking toward his next book where he would try again: "It [*Babbitt*] is satiric, rather more than *Main Street*; and for that reason I think—I hope—that the novel after *Babbitt* will be definitely non-satiric—except, of course, for occasional passages."[5] That Babbitt remains a type, a caricature, in spite of Lewis's efforts to make him complex, is what some critics find deficient in what they otherwise recognize as Lewis's most brilliant novel.[6]

Much of the differentiation among the various babbitts depended upon Lewis's handling of the tone of voice of his characters. Lewis was haunted by the voices of salesmen, managers, businessmen, and boosters. Self-exposure—the method of his satire—is accomplished by speeches in which his characters give their ignorance away. We know from William Rose Benét's reminiscence (quoted earlier) that Lewis practiced his mimicry in California as early as 1909. About that time, Lewis was working on his first novel, *Our Mr. Wrenn.* When it appeared in 1914, *Wrenn* contained some early and crude versions of the babbitt-voice, with the ineffectual hesitancies and the clichés which were to characterize it.

The handling of the tone, opinions, and character of Eddie Schwirtz, the paint salesman in *The Job,* was a significant development in Lewis's portraiture. Before his voice takes over (for, after the first pages of his initial appearance, we do not see Eddie; we hear him—and at great length), he is described as forty and red-faced, with a clipped mustache, a derby hat, and an uneven tie. When he and Una Golden are hiking and he feels the stirrings of love, he says, "I'm a poor old rough-neck, . . . but to-day, up here with you, I feel so darn good that I almost think I'm a decent citizen. Honest, little sister, I haven't felt so bully for a blue moon" (p. 210). In such a speech one finds the elements of all the babbitt-voices yet to come—that rather unreal overloading of clichés, the "manly" diction ("rough-neck," "so darn good") which is ultimately weak and mindless. I believe that Lewis is suggesting that clichés are the only words a babbitt-type dare use to express emotions, which the Schwirtzes and Babbitts fear. Their misunderstanding of emotion is what makes them comic, grotesque, or dangerous. Yet there is a curious little passage that comes a few pages later in *The Job,* where Schwirtz speaks in a strangely natural and affecting way; it contains much potential for a humanizing of Babbitt and Paul Riesling and Dodsworth, though Lewis used it only occasionally. Eddie tells Una about the death of his wife: "My wife died a year later. I couldn't get over it; seemed like I could have killed myself when I thought of any mean thing I might have said to her—not meaning anything, but hasty-like, as a man will. Couldn't seem to get over it. Evenings were just hell; they were so—empty. Even when I was out on the road, there wasn't anybody to write to, anybody that *cared* . . ." (p. 213). It is as if for a moment Lewis has heard the cadences of Jim or Huck. But there is nothing like it again in *The Job* and not enough of it elsewhere in Lewis.

The voice of George F. Babbitt introduces an important new tone that results from fatigue and is expressed in whining and self-pity.

The fatigue has been caused by deep discontent. Babbitt, who thinks of himself as the very backbone of America, is given to weak hesitations and ineffectual curses and commands. At the opening of the novel our Ideal Citizen is talking to himself, as he struggles with the toothpaste in the bathroom: "Verona been at it again! 'Stead of sticking to Lilidol, like I've re-peat-ed-ly asked her, she's gone and gotten some confounded stickum stuff that makes you sick!" (p. 5). Her "stickum stuff" is too feminine for a regular guy like Babbitt, but the triviality of the matter and his inability to make his daughter do as he wishes belie his picture of himself. Then self-pity overcomes him: "He was raging, 'By golly, here they go and use up all the towels, every doggone one of 'em, and they use 'em and get 'em all wet and sopping, and never put out a dry one for me—of course, . . . I'm the only person in the doggone house that's got the slightest doggone bit of consideration for other people and thoughtfulness and consider there may be others that may want to use the doggone bathroom after me and consider—'" (p. 6). His ineffectuality is shown not only in the weak profanity, but more importantly in the wasted words of his redundancies.

Babbitt sees himself as friendly, affable, and masculine, yet the he-man is soon fretting about the effect of banana fritters upon his digestion. He sees himself as imposed upon, for he works hard and ought to be rewarded with peace of mind. "I may not be any Rockefeller or James J. Shakespeare, but I certainly do know my own mind, and I do keep right on plugging along in the office and—" (p. 12). This man who knows his own mind relies upon the editorials of his newspaper, upon the sermons at his church, and upon the speeches he hears at his Boosters Club meetings in order to know what to think. To his daughter's expression of a desire to do social work, Babbitt gropes for words, stumbling and sputtering out clichés:

> "Now you look here! The first thing you got to understand is that all this uplift and flipflop and settlement-work and recreation is nothing in God's world but the entering wedge for socialism. The sooner a man learns he isn't going to be coddled, and he needn't expect a lot of free grub and, uh, all these free classes and flipflop and doodads for his kids unless he earns 'em, why, the sooner he'll get on the job and produce—produce—produce! That's what the country needs, and not all this fancy stuff that just enfeebles the will-power of the working man and gives his kids a lot of notions above their class" (p. 17).

Midway in his speech he fizzles, so he resorts to repetition of "flipflop and doodads." Suddenly he remembers an editorial: "get on the job and produce–produce–produce!" He has moved a long way from a simple response to his daughter's remark. In such ineffectual language does he challenge the world of business and politics.

Although Lewis's plans for the characterization of Babbitt resulted from his desire to create a rounded figure, displaying interior as well as exterior vision, Babbitt's character was to begin, Lewis wrote his publisher in December 1920, in the man's typicality; he is to be "the typical T. B. M. [tired business man], the man you hear drooling in the Pullman smoker."[7] But, Lewis went on, "having once so seen him, I want utterly to develop him so that he will seem not just typical but an individual." Discontentment was to be the principal device for suggesting Babbitt's inner self. Tired of the work routine, Babbitt "would like for once the flare of romantic love, the satisfaction of having left a mark on the city, and a let-up in his constant warring on competitors." But "only for a little while is he discontented, though." Babbitt is to surprise the reader by breaking away from the standards–a little.

How did Lewis plan to make Babbitt come alive? First, Babbitt's typicality, as Lewis saw it, must be extracted from hundreds of observations of individuals. Lewis's work through 1920 had prepared him to know what the man in the smoking car sounded like when he spoke. Nevertheless, Lewis did considerable research for this book, visiting Cincinnati and other cities of two, three, and four hundred thousand people. From his notes, he was able to put into the book a mass of accurate detail about clothes, houses, furnishings, cars, clubs, real estate enterprises, and conventions. Therefore, we have great confidence in Babbitt's typicality in respect to things and opinions: his toothpaste and bath-towels, his gray suit and his spectacles, the contents of his pockets, his Booster's Club button; and his indecisive and inconclusive discussion with his wife Myra about the choice of suits, his concern for his stomach, the opinions he gleans from his newspaper's editorials, his scorn for socialist agitators, and his faith in the strength of the towers of Zenith–all these observations we are delighted to recognize as true. The contradictions in his opinions ring true also: "We got no business interfering with the Irish or any other foreign government"; still, "it's beyond me why we don't just step in there [Russia] and kick those Bolshevik cusses out."

But during the account of the first two hours of Babbitt's day, Lewis plants evidence of the discontentment which is intended to reveal the interior Babbitt. It begins with irritability about the wet towels in the bathroom and the little chunks of toast and the socialist threat and his rebellious and bickering children. Soon, so early in the day, we hear the great burst of fatigue: "Oh, Lord, sometimes I'd like to quit the whole game. And the office worry and detail just as bad. And I act cranky and—I don't mean to, but I get—So darn tired!" (p. 23).

He says much the same thing before lunch, during lunch, after lunch, and in the evening. As the day ends, "his feet were loud on the steps as he clumped upstairs at the end of this great and treacherous day of veiled rebellions" (p. 94). To his friend Paul Riesling he had complained,

> "I don't know what's the matter with me to-day. . . . Kind of comes over me: here I've pretty much done all the things I ought to; supported my family, and got a good house and a six-cylinder car, and built up a nice little business, and I haven't any vices 'specially, except smoking. . . . I belong to the church, and play enough golf to keep in trim, and I only associate with good decent fellows. And yet, even so, I don't know that I'm entirely satisfied!" (pp. 60–61).

In this little speech, we have what I think is the essential insight of the book. Lewis gives us the babbitt-vision of the American Dream. Babbitt has lived according to its inspiration, but it is a dream which leaves the dreamer restless and betrayed.

Paul Riesling believes that there is a widespread undercurrent of dissatisfaction among businessmen; they seem content, yet one-third of them feel restless and won't admit it, while another third are simply miserable and know it. "They hate the whole peppy, boosting, go-ahead game, and they're bored by their wives and think their families are fools" (pp. 64–65).

Lewis has discovered that a babbitt can suffer the tensions of conformity, though conformity was not supposed to bring tension. A part of Babbitt's early-morning fatigue comes from indecisions and contradictions. So sensitive is he to marginal differences that deciding what suit to wear is an exhausting problem with many subtleties. Then he engages in a discussion with his wife which (though I shall abbreviate it) takes him through confusions like these:

> "I feel kind of punk this morning. . . . You oughtn't to serve those heavy banana fritters."
>
> "But you asked me to have some."
>
> "I know, but—. . . it would be a good thing for both of us if we took lighter lunches."
>
> "But Georgie, here at home I always do have a light lunch."

> "Mean to imply I make a hog of myself, eating down-town? . . . Why don't you serve more prunes at breakfast? . . ."
> "The last time I had prunes you didn't eat them" (pp. 10–11).

Such an exchange would indeed be wearing. Babbitt's fatigue engages both our sense of humor and our pity. It is both sound psychological insight and effective social criticism.

There is the additional tension of social-climbing: the Babbitts would like to enter the higher social level of the rich. At Babbitt's party, he and his friends congratulate themselves, however, on having reached the metropolitan middle-class ("those Main Street burgs are slow"). Beyond the satire of the party itself, which is excellent ("these small towns . . . all got an ambition that in the long run is going to make 'em the finest spots on earth—they all want to be just like Zenith"), Lewis reveals Babbitt's sense of guilt in having left the home village (pp. 117–19). And there is tension caused by contradictions in business practices. "The whole of the Glen Oriole project was a suggestion that Babbitt, though he really did hate men recognized as swindlers, was not too unreasonably honest." But, Lewis continues, "Babbitt was virtuous. He advocated, though he did not practise, the prohibition of alcohol; he praised, though he did not obey, the laws against motor-speeding; he paid his debts; he contributed to the church, the Red Cross, and the Y.M.C.A.; he followed the custom of his clan and cheated only as it was sanctified by precedent" (pp. 45–46). In the next scene, Lewis shows us Babbitt swindling a helpless storekeeper. The Puritan business ethic encourages pragmatic decisions which then fatigue the conscience.

Babbitt also frets over the problem of faithfulness to the wife he takes no interest in. "In twenty-three years of married life he had peered uneasily at every graceful ankle, every soft shoulder; in thought he had treasured them; but not once had he hazarded respectability by adventuring" (p. 37). Now he is restless and discontented. He dreams of a fairy-girl, a divine playmate. He is worried, too, about his relationships with his employees: "He liked to like the people about him; he was dismayed when they did not like him. . . . He was afraid of his still-faced clerks" (p. 72).

If these tensions disturb the private Babbitt, what of the public image of the Solid American Citizen? Babbitt's speech before the Real Estate Board describes his vision of himself. Lewis's parody is his means of attacking attitudes he detests:

"Our Ideal Citizen—I picture him first and foremost as being busier than a bird-dog, not wasting a lot of good time in day-dreaming or going to sassiety teas or kicking about things that are none of his business, but putting the zip into some store or profession or art. At night he lights up a good cigar, and climbs into the little old 'bus, and maybe cusses the carburetor, and shoots out home. He mows the lawn, or sneaks in some practice putting, and then he's ready for dinner. After dinner he tells the kiddies a story, or takes the family to the movies, or plays a few fists of bridge, or reads the evening paper, and a chapter or two of some good lively Western novel if he has a taste for literature, and maybe the folks next-door drop in. . . . Then he goes happily to bed, his conscience clear, having contributed his mite to the prosperity of the city and to his own bank-account" (pp. 181–82).

Yet in reality Babbitt sleeps fitfully and dreams of escape and rebellion.

On page 303 (with one-fourth of the novel remaining) Babbitt meets the socialist Seneca Doane, who recalls that in college Babbitt was "a liberal, sensitive chap," who had dreamed that he would become a lawyer, assume the causes of the poor, and fight the rich. With Doane's encouragement, Babbitt's overt rebellion begins. His quixotism stirs. He will draw strength from Nature; he will seek a princess outside of marriage; he will defend honesty in business and support social reform; he will right wrongs. But powerful forces are at work to call the quixotic adventurer and reformer back home:

Vast is the power of cities to reclaim the wanderer. More than mountains or the shore-devouring sea, a city retains its character, imperturbable, cynical, holding behind apparent changes its essential purpose. Though Babbitt had deserted his family and dwelt with Joe Paradise in the wilderness, though he had become a liberal, though he had been quite sure, on the night before he reached Zenith, that neither he nor the city would be the same again, ten days after his return he could not believe that he had ever been away. Nor was it at all evident to his acquaintances that there was a new George F. Babbitt (p. 308).

His friends note only a mild liberalism and a flicker of conscience. Both, however, worry them. They think him merely a crank at first. Then they decide to drive him out of their society or make him return. He becomes afraid of the terrorism of Vergil Gunch and the Good Citizens' League. When he comes back to the fold, however, a different terror remains with him—the terror of defeat: "They've licked me."

Lewis had planned from the beginning that Babbitt would break away from the standard "only for a little while." For all his careful planting of discontentments and tensions, Lewis had decided not to give Babbitt much sensitivity or intelligence. He was conceived of as a generic figure; Lewis had early pledged to have everyone soon talking of babbittry. It is impossible, however, to read Babbitt's last speech—his advice to his son to do what he wants to do—without realizing that Lewis had allowed Babbitt to know to a small extent what his experience of rebellion has meant. But George is still very much a babbitt, frightened, guilty, and conformist, and both his way of addressing his son and that son's character itself leave little confidence of growth. "Yet we *like* Babbitt," writes Professor Sheldon Grebstein, "and are indulgent of him, just as Lewis is and intends." The book, he goes on, "is the outstanding social satire of its generation, if not of American literature."[8] Howell Daniels believes that the novel is admirable because Lewis has brought Babbitt fully before us by means of the rendering of his past and his "capacity for wonder," conveyed "in a prose which moves easily between Babbitt's world of fact and the world of fantasy."[9]

So much babbitt-talk derived from such popular media as editorials, westerns, films, and romantic fiction; Babbitt's desire to escape into a mock-Thoreauvian wilderness; and the importance of the glorious princess of his dreams as embodied in Tanis Judique—these give to Lewis's novel a pattern by which he can challenge middle-class society in America. *Babbitt* is a remarkable book, in large part because of Lewis's parodies of conversation, oratory, and print, which open to us, through exposures of the corruptions of language, the parallel faults of society.

Chapter 8

Arrowsmith

Lewis admired the laboratory researcher and made use of much of the researcher's method in his extensive and careful fieldwork and note-taking as preparation for his novels. Research would restrain the idler's fantasizing. Furthermore, the researcher is both objectively removed from life and ultimately useful to it. Lewis feared being useless: not the idle but the industrious apprentice was he, not the dilettante or bohemian but the eight-hours-a-day professional writer. Hard work was the pioneer way, and whatever reading, thinking, dreaming young Lewis had needed to do—though they might look to his townspeople like time-wasting—were but the prelude to the hard and useful labor which would follow. These fears and justifications became a credo, declared in 1921. Though overblown, pretentious, and even embarrassing to read, it is an important statement of his attitude:

> The builder, and he may be a builder in business as much as in any art, concentrates on his building, yet sees all of life expanding, as circle beyond circle of possible achievement is disclosed. He will neither whine, "I can't find time," nor, at the other extreme, will he pound his own back and bellow, "Oh, I'm one grand little worker." His idol is neither the young man sighing over a listless pipe, nor the human calliope. He works, persistently, swiftly, without jar.[1]

Not the least interesting phrase here is the one which suggests that art can be "built." But of greater importance in the credo is the rapid evocation of certain character types. Neither a whiner nor a bellower be; much of Lewis's satirical characterization is an excoriation of whiners and bellowers, who appear as bohemians, preachers, and salesmen. Such types arose to the front of his consciousness from his experience of life—in the village, at Yale, on a cattleboat to England, in a socialistic utopian community, in Greenwich Village, in the offices of New York publishing houses. To oppose them, Lewis drew portraits of the "builders"—engineers and architects—some of whom he tried as best he could to make significantly alert to circles of meaningful achievement. If the voice of one human being echoes within him, it surely must be that of his conscientious and puritanical father, the man who worked hard and always paid his debts.

While still working on *Babbitt,* Lewis wrote his publisher that he was planning to make his next novel "not satiric at all; rebellious as ever, perhaps, but the central character *heroic.*"[2] He added that he was already getting gleams for it. What he was specifically getting gleams for was the labor novel which he never wrote. Instead, he wrote *Arrowsmith,* which was the result of a meeting he had soon afterward with Dr. Paul de Kruif in which Lewis recognized at once that the story of a medical researcher offered, in a way congenial to him, the kind of heroic material he had been seeking.

While he worked on *Arrowsmith,* Lewis was more enthusiastic than he had ever been before: "I am quite sure that it will be much better than either *Main St* or *Babbitt;* the characters have more life to me, more *stir.*"[3] He said that he thought the new book would be the meatiest of all, in respect to character, places, contrasting purposes and views of life.[4] It was also the novel into which Lewis felt he had put the best of himself. All his "respect for learning, for integrity, for accuracy, and for the possibilities of human achievement," he said, were to be found in the portrait of Professor Max Gottlieb. And most of his "capacity for loyalty to love and friendship" had gone into the character of Leora Tozer, Arrowsmith's wife.[5] Elsewhere Lewis said that Dr. Sondelius was the favorite among all his characters.[6] Finally the identification of himself with Dr. Martin Arrowsmith—physician and bacteriological researcher—is symbolized in Lewis's title of a mock obituary of himself: "The Death of Arrowsmith."

Arrowsmith, like most of Lewis's other novels, is a tale of a quixote. From the opening, Martin Arrowsmith is a wanderer, a fancifier, a romantic. He searches for the common sense aspect of himself, for some outward figures who can encourage his control over romance and keep him at his work, and for a basis upon which to criticize those fools, clowns, hypocrites, and exploiters he encounters in various heroic engagements. The material out of which Arrowsmith's mind and values were created is that of popular fiction.

Judging from the otherwise unnecessary opening section to the book, it appears as if Lewis took very seriously his intention to give the story broad heroic, perhaps mythic, scope. The spirit of Arrowsmith had pioneer sources. We see his great-grandmother, a ragged girl of fourteen, crossing the country on a wagon, her father sick, her mother dead, and her younger brothers and sisters clamoring about her. The old man says, "Ye better turn." "We're going on," she replies with pioneer courage, "jus' long as we can. Going West! They's a whole lot of new things I aim to be seeing!" (p. 1). She is on the road; she seeks adventure: she suggests the union of the metaphors of the quixote and the pioneer.

In addition to pioneer ancestry, Arrowsmith possesses an epic blood-line: German, French, Scotch, Irish, Spanish, a mixture Lewis labels "Jewish," and a great deal of English, "which is itself a combination of Primitive Britain, Celt, Phoenician, Roman, German, Dane, and Swede" (p. 2). Arrowsmith's parentage is shrouded like that of the hero of tradition; his father and mother neither appear nor are ever talked of nor remembered by the son.

It is not from family that Arrowsmith learns the values of life, but from three mentors—Doc Vickerson, Max Gottlieb, and Terry Wickett. The first mentor appears only in Chapter One. There is a fuss made about a symbolic gift of a "beloved magnifying glass" that Doc gives to Arrowsmith, but the glass is never recalled thereafter. Yet it is significant that the Arrowsmith who has pioneer blood in his veins should begin his quest with inspiration from Lewis's typically American pariah, the defeated bachelor-drunkard-agnostic who is nevertheless keen, inquiring, independent. Soon enough Vickerson is supplanted by Professor Gottlieb, both more brilliant and more filled with doubt. As a Jew and a European, he is trying to find his way in an alien culture. Lastly, from Wickett, the representative of the new scientific yet cynical vigor of America, Arrowsmith learns how to escape from the frustrations of society to a primitive sanctuary in nature. In this novel, then, we come to Lewis's attempt to create a hero—that is (in Caroline Gordon's words), a person who answers some call to action, who seems to unite and portray certain trends of his age.[7] It is a quixotic hero that Lewis creates, but one not any the less representative for all that.

Although the reader should not lose sight of the book's pretentious beginnings, soon a human story unfolds. Lewis speaks of Arrowsmith, not as a giant, but as a young man "who regarded himself as a seeker after truth yet who stumbled and slid back all his life and bogged himself in every obvious morass" (p. 44). Now on this level we have the man of science as essentially an ordinary man, plain, simple, unintellectual, and bungling, "full of hasty faults and of perverse honesty; a young man often unkindly, often impolite." But he had one gift—his curiosity (p. 308).

We are not given lengthy book-lists that suggest how reading has affected Arrowsmith's mind, but we see some later book choices that tell us what kinds of reading he has an affinity for. Arrowsmith is but half-educated, we are told. To remedy the defect, he reads Robert Service, European history, *The Golden Bowl* ("which an unfortunate schoolteacher had left"), and Conrad, from whom he feeds his fancy (as we might expect), not his moral being: "as [Arrowsmith] drove the prairie roads, he was marching into jungle villages—sun helmets, orchids, lost temples of obscene and dog-faced deities, secret and sun-scarred rivers" (pp. 170–71). During the miseries of the pregnancy of his wife Leora, to soothe their troubled minds "he read to her, not history now and Henry James but 'Mrs. Wiggs of the Cabbage Patch,' which both of them esteemed a very fine tale" (p. 173).

Yet later in New York, Arrowsmith reads "the classics of physical science: Copernicus and Galileo, Lavoisier, Newton, LaPlace, Descartes, Faraday. He became completely bogged in Newton's 'Fluxions'" (p. 300). Are these names just amusing counters for Lewis? The books seem to make little impression upon his hero. Furthermore, at no point in the progress of the novel does Arrowsmith's manner of speaking change; always it is the talk of an exuberant boy. To the pregnant Leora he says soothingly, "Golly, we—No, not 'golly.' Well, what *can* you say except 'golly'?" and he goes on to promise travel to "Italy and all those places. All those old narrow streets and old castles! There must be scads of 'em" (p. 173).

The novel is laced with quixotism beyond the castles of Italy. Arrowsmith declares his quixotic intentions at the outset: "I'm going to have them all"—fame, women, adventure (he will "see the world"). One summer, when he is working as a telephone lineman, he has a vision:

> He was atop a pole and suddenly, for no clear cause, his eyes opened and he saw; as though he had just awakened he saw that the prairie was vast, that the sun was kindly on rough pasture and ripening wheat, on the old horses, the easy, broad-beamed, friendly horses, and on his red-faced jocose companions; he saw that the meadow larks were jubilant, and blackbirds shining by little pools, and with the living sun all life was living (pp. 31–32).

His girl friend, Madeline Fox, seems a sister of Carol Kennicott in her own fancying: "She compared her refuge to the roof of a Moorish palace, to a Spanish patio, to a Japanese garden, to a 'pleasaunce of old Provençal'" (p. 47).

Then Lewis, the fantasist, takes flight. Arrowsmith meets Leora Tozer, who will become his bride shortly. There is a rhapsodic passage during their first meeting:

> Sound of mating birds, sound of spring blossoms dropping in the tranquil air, the bark of sleepy dogs at midnight; who is to set them down and make them anything but hackneyed? And as natural, as conventional, as youthfully gauche, as eternally beautiful and authentic as those ancient sounds was the talk of Martin and Leora in that passionate half-hour when each found in the other a part of his own self, always vaguely missed, discovered now with astonished joy. They rattled like hero and heroine of a sticky tale, like sweat-shop operatives, like bouncing rustics, like prince and princess (pp. 55–56).

After being dismissed from the university, Arrowsmith takes to wandering:

> Always, in America, there remains from pioneer days a cheerful pariahdom of shabby young men who prowl causelessly from state to state, from gang to gang, in the power of the Wanderlust. They wear black sateen shirts, and carry bundles. They are not permanently tramps. They have home towns to which they return, to work quietly in the factory or the section-gang for a year—for a week—and as quietly to disappear again. . . . Into that world of voyageurs Martin vanished (p. 97).

Furthermore as an intern he is involved in soap opera episodes like the one in which he attends to the victims of a fire: "They heard the blang-blang-blang of a racing ambulance, incessant, furious, defiant. Without orders, the crowd opened, and through them, almost grazing them, slid the huge gray car. At the back, haughty in white uniform, nonchalant on a narrow seat, was The Doctor—Martin Arrowsmith." (p. 117). He rushes to an unconscious youngster who has inhaled too much smoke. A reporter approaches Arrowsmith. "'Will he pull through, Doc?' he twanged. 'Sure, I think so. Suffocation. Heart's still going.' Martin yelped the last words from the step at the back of the ambulance" (p. 118).

But whatever Lewis shows us in dialogue and action, his exposition insists upon Arrowsmith's growth and maturity. "While Martin developed in a jagged way from the boy of Wheatsylvania to mature man, his relations to Leora developed from loyal boy-and-girl adventurousness to lasting solidity" (p. 272). Yet shortly thereafter we read, "He was sobbing, with her head on his shoulder, 'Oh, you poor, scared, bullied kid, trying to be grownup.'" Can we overlook the slick-magazine language of such passages? I think not. Here is a section in which Arrowsmith diverts himself with Orchid Pickerbaugh, aged nineteen: "One day when Orchid came swarming all over the laboratory and perched on the bench with a whisk of stockings, he stalked to her, masterfully seized her wrists, and kissed her as she deserved to be kissed." He is at once frightened; she is shocked. "He kissed her again. She yielded and for a moment there was nothing in the universe" (p. 233).

This novel, with its serious theme, has been acclaimed as Lewis's best work. Nevertheless, in view of the passages which I have been examining and the protagonist who is emerging from them, I find its heroic pretension embarrassing, unless the hero be thought of as a quixote. Otherwise, one episode after another of the book "freezes up our credulity and provokes our fiercest denial," as Allen Tate has said of another novel.[8] In New York, when Arrowsmith hits upon something significant, we are shown his frenzy and exhaustion as he rushes to consult the library, as he experiments, as he takes notes, neglects Leora, ignores even his weariness. His language at such moments is impulsive and chaotic. He forgets Gottlieb's advice to be calm. "God, woman, I've got it! The real big stuff! I've found something, not a chemical you put in I mean, that eats bugs—dissolves 'em—kills 'em. May be a big new step in therapeutics. Oh, no, rats, I don't suppose it really is. Prob'ly just another of my bulls" (p. 312). He sobs to Leora, "Oh, I couldn't do anything without you! Don't ever leave me! I do love you so, even if this damned work does keep me tied up" (p. 313). He becomes sick with nervous exhaustion. He is never far from hysteria. If medical researchers do not in fact act so wildly, as one commentator will argue later, many readers were apparently swept up by Lewis's picture of the hero at work.

Nowhere is Arrowsmith so confused, so innocent, and so idealistic as in his relationships with women; in this regard, as in the bent of his mind toward science, he is indeed a spiritual offspring of such quixotes as Hawk Ericson and Milt Daggett. By the writing of this book, Lewis had altered his ideas about women, however. He had found sinister elements in the eager young feminists who wished only for self-realization. They had metamorphosed from the idealized Ruth Winslow and Claire Boltwood, from the more determined Una Golden, into the nervously reformist and uncertain Carol Kennicott. By *Arrowsmith* Lewis was bitterly portraying women he called "Improvers."

Arrowsmith becomes involved with four women who reflect important aspects of the novel's message: Madeline Fox, Leora Tozer, Orchid Pickerbaugh, and Joyce Lanyon. Lewis gathers the good qualities of women into the much-admired portrait of Leora Tozer. To Orchid Pickerbaugh he ascribes immature frivolity. He displays shallow pretension, finickiness and uselessness in Madeline Fox and Joyce Lanyon. By the time he wrote *Arrowsmith*, Lewis had become so antagonistic to such "princesses" as Ruth and Claire that he could editorialize that "few women can for long periods keep from trying to Improve their men, and to Improve means to change a person from what he is, whatever that may be, into something else" (p. 46). Such women cannot be restrained. Young Arrowsmith falls in love with Madeline, who is an Improver. But shortly thereafter he meets one of the few women in Lewis's fiction who are not Improvers —the most praised woman in all of Lewis's books, the compliant, self-effacing, and loyal Leora Tozer. With her, Arrowsmith felt "an instant and complete comradeship . . . free from the fencing and posing of his struggle with Madeline." Leora "was full of laughter at humbugs." Furthermore, "she was feminine but undemanding; she was never Improving and rarely shocked" (pp. 55–57).

Arrowsmith finds himself engaged to both girls. An important choice must be made between the Improver and the Companion. To demonstrate the differences, Lewis arranges a scene in which Arrowsmith naïvely and quixotically brings the two girls together. Madeline reacts badly (for which, if for nothing else, she ought to be excused—it's a rather foolish thing the hero does, though it is indicative of Lewis's sense of romantic drama); she stalks out. Leora understands and remains (pp. 64–70).

But the spirit of Madeline the Improver does not leave the story. It returns in the body of Joyce Lanyon some 315 pages later. During the plague episode, Arrowsmith encounters Joyce, whom he sees as his transforming vision must. She must be his sister, he thinks. "She was perhaps thirty to his thirty-seven, but in her slenderness, her paleness, her black brows and dusky hair, she was his twin; she was his self enchanted" (p. 384). Arrowsmith's analysis is faulty, however, the result of his ever-active fancy. Joyce revives the spirit of Madeline. Yet after Leora dies of the plague, Arrowsmith marries Joyce. With plenty of time and opportunity to observe her, Arrowsmith walks straight into marriage with an Improving Woman: "An Arranger and even an Improver was Joyce," we are told by the author before the marriage occurs (p. 411), and we readers have no information about Joyce that is unknown to the hero. She declares to him, "I do like pretty people and gracious manners and good games." She is a woman who likes to play; she says so. But there is an important difference to note in the author's treatment of the matter here. At this point in his development, play has unpleasant connotations. The notion of play has become attached to the Arranger, the Improver, the Nag. This attitude, which had begun to appear in the treatment of Carol Kennicott, who had the urge to improve the town, is fully formulated in Joyce Lanyon. From this point on, women who want to play do not receive the author's sympathy.

Joyce and her kind contrast with Leora, who obeyed Arrowsmith's wishes and understood "without his saying them all the flattering things he planned to say." But not so with Joyce: "She could, she said, kill a man who considered her merely convenient furniture." "She expected him to remember her birthday, her taste in wine, her liking for flowers, and her objection to viewing the process of shaving. She wanted a room to herself; she insisted that he knock before entering" (p. 414). Arrowsmith believes that he has made himself the slave of Joyce. He decides to escape from her. With startling callousness, he leaves his son as well as Joyce herself. As he retreats to a shack in the Vermont woods, he kisses their infant son and mutters, "Come to me when you grow up, old man" (p. 443).

William Wrenn and Hawk Ericson each had a choice between two women. Now in *Arrowsmith* such a choice re-emerges as an important element in the form of Lewis's books. Madeline Fox and Joyce Lanyon, standing at the opening and the close of the novel, can symbolize grasping and selfish impulses in our society, while Leora Tozer represents generous and considerate ones. Arrowsmith can do his best work only in the atmosphere of Leora, or alone. For Leora had borne the tedium of Arrowsmith's work without complaint. "She sat quiet (a frail child, only up to one's shoulder, not nine minutes older than at marriage, nine years before), or she napped inoffensively, in the long living-room of their flat, while he worked" (p. 300). But she does more than bear the tedium. Her baby dies, and one suspects that its death is a convenience that keeps Arrowsmith unburdened by responsibility. She overlooks his faults and indiscretions and never interferes with his work. Leora's death, which occurs by accident during the plague at St. Hubert, suggests that Lewis may have wished to lay an extra affliction upon Arrowsmith so that he will be forced to retreat from the world. Arrowsmith's remorse is silence; he displays no guilt at all, though he had abandoned her at a lodge on the island, where she contracts the disease. After her death, he marries Joyce. How slow to learn Lewis's male characters are! They seem to need one extra demonstration of truths they should know but somehow cannot accept—and this need for an extra demonstration causes an impatience with the structure of his books at the same time that it suggests some tragic overtones of the hero who cannot change. In *Main Street* and in *Arrowsmith,* as in *Dodsworth* and *Cass Timberlane,* which follow later, the extra demonstration, actually a repetition of something already clear to the reader, lengthens the book. Of the best work Lewis did, only *Babbitt* has no such repetition and only *Babbitt* is as tight a novel as any of the others might have been, to their benefit.

The theme of *Arrowsmith* is that the frauds, wastrels, and hypocrites of American life divert a man from his best, purest work and that his only salvation is retreat. There is no place for Arrowsmith in McGurk Institute or in Joyce's circle of friends, or anywhere else in America. This book is Lewis's most comprehensive testing of American environments. In its course Arrowsmith ventures across the nation, from the village of Wheatsylvania, North Dakota, to the small city of Nautilus, to the middle-sized midwestern city of Zenith, to Chicago, and to New York. Everywhere he is rejected and everywhere he rejects. Everywhere self-realization is stifled and idealism is defiled. He resolves these by withdrawal. To justify his retreat, Arrowsmith enunciates his code of the pioneers. He says that the objection that there is a responsibility to one's family has been what has kept "almost everybody, all these centuries, from being anything but a machine for digestion and propagation and obedience" (p. 443). Very few men ever "willingly leave a soft bed for a shanty bunk in order to be pure . . . and those of us that are pioneers—" He stops, and the word *pioneer* recalls not only the book's opening passages but one of Lewis's controlling ideas.

Carl Van Doren thought that "there is something true to an honored American tradition in Arrowsmith's retirement," something that reminded him of Daniel Boone and Leatherstocking.[9] But Warren Beck, who finds Arrowsmith "a crude and lopsided human being," has said that this retreat which frees Arrowsmith "of feminine domination, social intrusions, or even any friction with colleagues" means that "the terms under which Arrowsmith succeeds are thus less significant, humanly speaking, than those under which Babbitt failed."[10] Some readers believe, then, that Arrowsmith's retreat in the name of the pioneer spirit is but a further excuse for one of Lewis's boy-men never to mature. Bernard DeVoto, who said that "Martin suffers from arrested development" and "is a fool,"[11] noted further that "his customary state of mind while working at his trade has caused a bacteriologist of my acquaintance to want—I use his own winning expression—to puke."[12] A Harvard bacteriologist has written: "If an epidemologist on a plague study talked and behaved in the manner of the hero of *Arrowsmith,* he would be regarded as something of a yellow ass and a nuisance by his associates."[13]

Yet in the book there is also Gottlieb to uphold the ideal of the scientific attitude. In Gottlieb Lewis mixed dignity and genius and flaws in a more fully realized characterization. To Arrowsmith he had given nothing like Gottlieb's sense of sorrow nor his vision of the potential achievement of the human race nor his cynicism. Gottlieb has the task of expressing the themes of the book. It is he who voices the despair about the failures of human accomplishment. It is he who suggests that in the scientific approach lies the hope of the future. Significantly, Gottlieb makes no withdrawal from the world until his final illness, but continues his work in spite of heavy miseries which he suffers. Lewis surrounds Gottlieb in mystery. If Gottlieb is at the opening a fabulous and legendary character ("It was said that he could create life in the laboratory" [p. 9]) and if Arrowsmith first sees him as "a tall figure, ascetic, self-contained, apart . . . unconscious of the world . . ." and "romantic as a cloaked horseman" (pp. 10–11), yet when Arrowsmith later comes to his office, he sees Gottlieb as "testy and middle-aged," with wrinkles, "a man who had headaches, who became agonizingly tired, who could be loved" (p. 13). Gottlieb is cynical about most of his students—they are "potatoes." But to some few students he can teach "the ultimate lesson of science, which is to wait and doubt" (p. 12). Arrowsmith becomes a disciple.

A two-chapter interlude in the history of Arrowsmith's career fills out the characterization of Gottlieb (pp. 123–43). His plans for a research institution lead to his dismissal from the University of Winnemac. He then compromises his principles by taking a job with a commercial laboratory in Pittsburgh. In his misery Gottlieb turns to the Book of Job. Yet although we are led inward, here as so often elsewhere Lewis's fanciful notions mar the effect. Lewis imagines an unbelievable scene intended to give breadth to his characterization by pushing it to outer limits; instead, it interrupts the impact of his story. It seems that Gottlieb, "the placidly virulent hater of religious rites, had a religious-seeming custom." He would kneel by his bed and let his mind run free. "It was very much like prayer, though certainly there was no formal invocation, no consciousness of a Supreme Being—other than Max Gottlieb." The episode seems extravagant when we find that the subject of his prayer is "commercialism" (p. 136). Furthermore, there is nothing in *Job* nor in Jewish religious observance that would lead Gottlieb to perform the rite which Lewis reports to us—even taking fully into account that Gottlieb is not a practicing Jew and might even intend an affront to orthodoxy. At such crucial points in his characterization Lewis romanticizes. His reportorial technique fails to provide him with information; fabrication takes over.

Gottlieb, in spite of his misery, succeeds in producing anti-toxin in the test tube. The head of the commercial laboratory pressures him to give up verification and begin producing and marketing antitoxin at once. Gottlieb's older daughter runs off with a gambler; his son is worthless; his wife dies. It is a desperate moment. But suddenly and fortunately the McGurk Institute in New York City calls him to join its staff. At this point he leaves the novel for 132 pages. Then, having read an article by Arrowsmith, Gottlieb invites him to join the institute. Gottlieb speaks a famous passage, his statement of the religion of the scientist (pp. 277–80). The philanthropists, the doctors, the preachers, the manufacturers, the eloquent statesmen, and soft-hearted authors have made a mess of the world. "Maybe now it is time for the scientist, who works and searches and never goes around howling how he loves everybody!" Into this goes Lewis's Wellsian hope for salvation of the world through science. Gottlieb's advice is "Work twice as hard as you can, and keep people from using you. I will try to protect you from Success."

So inspired, Arrowsmith "prayed then the prayer of the scientist," a fantasy in inflated rhetoric, probably true to the character Lewis has created but embarrassing to anyone listening over Arrowsmith's shoulder: "God give me unclouded eyes and freedom from haste. God give me a quiet and relentless anger against all pretense and all pretentious work and all work left slack and unfinished. God give me a restlessness whereby I may neither sleep nor accept praise till my observed results equal my calculated results or in pious glee I discover and assault my error. God give me strength not to trust to God!" (pp. 280–81). Carl Van Doren found this prayer "Faustian" while Bernard DeVoto found it repulsive.[14] It seems boyish, if nothing else, and it might have been created under the inspiration of Kipling's "If."

After Martin discovers phage, Gottlieb, true to his science, cautions him that further proof be sought. When it is revealed that phage has been discovered in Europe, Gottlieb helps soothe this disappointment. "Martin, it iss nice that you will corroborate D'Hérelle. That is science: to work and not to care—too much—if somebody else gets the credit" (p. 327). This is the essence of Gottlieb's character and a deeper message than that of world-salvation through science. When Arrowsmith offers to test phage during a plague in St. Hubert, Gottlieb insists that he use the phage with only half the patients and keep the other as controls. Lewis adds a pathetic note to the departure: as Arrowsmith and his wife sail, they see Gottlieb at the pier, running to wave farewell, then, not finding them, turning sadly away. On his return to New York, Arrowsmith finds Gottlieb senile, unable to speak English, unable to recognize him. Arrowsmith had wanted forgiveness for the quixotic gesture of throwing over the scientific controls at St. Hubert and inoculating everyone so that he could not tell whether the serum had had any effect upon the subsiding of the plague. (Robert Morss Lovett wrote that the phenomena of the plague were sufficiently well known so that if all were inoculated and most survived, the cure *had* been found.[15]) Lewis adds, "Martin understood that never could he be punished now and cleansed. Gottlieb had sunk into his darkness still trusting him" (p. 403).

I find *Arrowsmith* a test of our response to the quixotic novel. In spite of my reservations about this book, much of it is admirable. There are satiric passages of great skill. The handling of Wheatsylvania, which I shall not recount, shows that Lewis had become even more deft at satirizing villages than he was in the creation of Gopher Prairie. A large gallery of doctors is exposed. But Arrowsmith himself is an exhibit of the American who never grows up, whose escape from a manipulative woman and a crushing social system seems less than estimable because he will take no responsibility for his child nor show grief for the bride who had served him.

Whatever the defects of the book, the hold that it has upon its readers is the result of Lewis's great energy. *Arrowsmith* overflows with energy—adolescent as it may seem at times. Whether we are watching Arrowsmith ride the ambulance to a fire or shout his joy at discovering a cure for plague, we are swept up by an energy that cannot be dismissed—a dedication to hard work and a rage for justice that are Lewis's special brazen, audacious qualities. *Arrowsmith* requires only that Lewis have perceived his hero with irony, with Cervantine distance so that the quixotic qualities that we have noticed could be read as mock heroics. Carried away by the injunction to create a hero, Lewis withholds the comic perspective from Arrowsmith and asks us to take Arrowsmith's quixotic reading, adventures, and enchantments quite seriously.

One can see how Lewis strove to move onward from *Babbitt* to what he intended as a heroic novel. His protagonist would be a common man engaged in a large enterprise. Lewis's method of extravagant gestures, leading to the plague at St. Hubert, would give the novel and its questing hero their symbolic power. He did, in fact, achieve much. But our disappointments come at those places where Lewis called to his aid the very excesses of fancy which he ought to have mocked. Lewis seemed to be caught by his ambivalence toward romance at precisely that moment when he was realizing the fulfillment of his ambitions.

Chapter 9

Mantrap and *Elmer Gantry*

Mantrap, a very poor novel that can be disposed of quickly, was brought out in 1926 and draws upon Lewis's experiences on a fishing trip to Canada. The protagonist, Ralph Prescott, is a weakly-conceived quixote who has "made his bow to Thoreau and Emerson and Ruskin." Much space is given to breaking stereotypes, many of them derived from fiction. The first one, for instance, occurs when the suggestion is made to attach an outboard motor to a canoe. Ralph is shocked, but his friend responds, "I suppose you expect 'em [Cree chiefs] to wear buckskin and paddle birch-bark canoes! Why, there isn't hardly a chief there that hasn't got an outboard motor and a white man's canvas canoe." Ralph's imagination is filled with visions of the North—"visions derived from the yarns which he absorbed in bed, after midnight. . . ." He has even fancied "a log cabin, and at the door a lovely Indian princess" (pp. 15–17). For Ralph "had been brought up on the Fenimore Cooper tradition of Indians. He expected all of them to look like the chieftain on the buffalo nickel" (p. 36). "They did not look in the least like lords of the wilderness [the door that screened the Chinese valet is opening again]. . . . They looked like undersized Sicilians who had been digging a sewer. . . . Feathers and blankets they wore not, but rusty black suits from the cheaper kind of white man's back-street shops" (p. 37).

Alverna Easter, the wife of a fishing guide, is somewhat like Carol Kennicott and something of a preview of Nande Azeredo in *Dodsworth*—alert, flirtatious, vulgar—"this manicure girl who was also Helen and Iseult and Héloïse" (p. 185). She has a closet full of clothes yet wears the khaki skirt, flannel shirt, and high laced boots "of a heroine in a Wild West melodrama" (p. 202). Lewis notes that "in fiction, all proper tenderfeet, particularly if they wear eyeglasses and weigh not over one hundred and thirty-seven pounds, after three weeks on a ranch, in a lumber-camp, or on a whaler become hardened and wise. Usually they beat the two-hundred-and-sixteen-pound bully and marry the boss's daughter" (p. 214). But this is not the experience Ralph is encountering.

Ralph and Alverna do run off—that is, they are guided off by Lawrence Jackfish, but Jackfish deserts them, and they are "two babes in the woods" (p. 253). Joe Easter rescues them, and resolution of the triangle that they have formed is for each one to go in his own direction—Alverna to Minneapolis, Joe to his woods, Ralph back to New York.

Earlier I suggested that whereas *Arrowsmith,* Lewis's great novel of the mid-twenties, was uncertain in its attitude toward quixotism, *The Sun Also Rises* has as one of its essential themes the rejection of the quixote, Robert Cohn. The fishing trip to Burguete is important in establishing the moral values implicit in Hemingway's realism. Jake and Bill exorcize quixotism by mocking the romanticism of A. E. W. Mason and the "irony and pity" of Anatole France, as well as William Jennings Bryan and such "dreamers" as Ford, Coolidge, and Rockefeller (pp. 112–25). The fishing itself is carefully rendered not only as a skill that testifies to one's manhood but as a control over and cure for one's despair. *Mantrap,* however, appearing in the same year as Hemingway's novel, fails in its representation of sport and leaves the rehabilitation of Ralph Prescott to a foolish adventure with a frivolous girl. We should not take this novel seriously—it seems a digression in the movement of Lewis's work—though it does illustrate Lewis's easy acquiescence in the temptations of fantasy at the expense of larger issues.

The angriest of Lewis's novels, *Elmer Gantry* seems to arise from impulses that invert the quixotic. Elmer, after all, is not an idealist; though he ventures forth, he does not do so in the name of chivalry; and, finally, he does not practice the transmuting powers of fancy. Nevertheless, it is possible to recognize the working of quixotic elements throughout the novel, especially in the fancifully conceived Sharon Falconer and in the character who is a foil for Elmer, Frank Shallard. The novel is absorbing, and I should like to say a few words about it.

What has educated Elmer (a few books, oratory, sermons, tracts, hymns, and a smattering of a college education) must be ridiculed in order to purge it from the land. Lewis's attack upon the villages—nowhere so embittered as in *Elmer Gantry*—occurs through exposure of the cultural opportunities which the village provides, and these are thin indeed. Most literary materials found in the village are reflections of American popular culture before the turn of the century. They were intended to feed the American dream, but instead fashioned the nightmare—out of books!

Elmer seems a demonic figure. He is out for money and pleasure and power—and the ministry is the career which gives him all three. He is a complete hypocrite and a complete opportunist. As Mark Schorer has pointed out, Elmer is rarely aware of himself as a hypocrite and achieves neither insight nor growth.[1] Nevertheless, Lewis supplies sufficient background to account for Elmer's going into the ministry.

Elmer himself had owned "two volumes of Conan Doyle, one of E. P. Roe, and a priceless copy of 'Only a Boy.'" His literary inspirations were McGuffey's Readers, Nick Carter, Bible stories, and such stock characters as "Little Lame Tom who shamed the wicked rich man that owned the handsome team of grays and the pot hat and led him to Jesus. The ship's captain who in the storm took counsel with the orphaned but righteous child of missionaries in Zomballa. The Faithful Dog who saved his master during a terrific conflagration . . ." (p. 26). (Later Elmer runs from a conflagration, saving no one but himself.)

Elmer's friend Jim Lefferts, a freethinker, has a somewhat wider list than Elmer: an encyclopedia, *Pickwick*, Swinburne, Ingersoll, and Paine. But in the house of Elmer's mistress, Lulu Bains, they sing and read "Seeing Nelly Home," "Old Black Joe," "Beulah Land," *Farm and Fireside,* and *Modern Priscilla* (pp. 108–109). When Elmer joins evangelist Sharon Falconer, he supplies poetry for her sermons, using Ella Wheeler Wilcox, James Whitcomb Riley, and Thomas Moore, with philosophy from Ralph Waldo Trine (p. 200). Bishop Toomis possesses a complete Dickens, a complete Walter Scott, Tennyson, Macaulay, Ruskin, Mrs. Humphrey Ward, Winston Churchill, Elizabeth of the German Garden, and books on travel and nature study: *How to Study the Birds, My Summer in the Rockies,* and *Pansies for Thoughts.* His mind was shaped most of all by his souvenirs of his travel-adventures. Some characters from Lewis even read Sinclair Lewis himself; the Reverend Philip McGarry asks his friend Frank Shallard to "forget that you have to make a new world, better'n the Creator's, right away tonight—you and Bernard Shaw and H. G. Wells and H. L. Mencken and Sinclair Lewis (Lord, how that book of Lewis', 'Main Street,' did bore me . . .)" (p. 371).

Lewis indicates the shaping of minds and values in such a village as Elmer's:

> The church and Sunday School at Elmer's village, Paris, Kansas, a settlement of nine hundred evangelical Germans and Vermonters . . . had been the center of all his emotions, aside from hell-raising, hunger, sleepiness, and love. And even these emotions were represented in the House of the Lord, in the way of tacks in pew-cushions, Missionary Suppers with chicken pie and angel's-food cake, soporific sermons, and the proximity of flexible little girls in thin muslin. But the arts and the sentiments and the sentimentalities—they were for Elmer perpetually associated only with the church (p. 25).

The church provided all the music he ever heard, his only oratory except for campaign speeches by politicians, all his painting and sculpture, and all his philosophic ideas. "In Bible stories, in the words of the great hymns, in the anecdotes which the various preachers quoted, he had his only knowledge of literature" (p. 26). Lewis exercises his bitterness against the failures of the church by making the church itself accountable for Elmer's being no better educated. His widowed mother was "owned by the church," we are told, and the fact that the boy was fatherless is less important than that the church could not provide Elmer with principles.

In his preparation for the ministry, it is ironic that Elmer plagiarizes his first (and most frequently useful) sermon from the social reformer Robert G. Ingersoll: "Love is the only bow on life's dark cloud. It is the Morning and the Evening Star. It shines upon the cradle of the babe, and sheds its radiance upon the quiet tomb . . ." (p. 57). As Elmer's career begins its ascent, we learn something more of the images which fill his mind:

> For all his slang, his cursing, his mauled plurals and singulars, Elmer had been compelled in college to read certain books, to hear certain lectures, all filled with flushed, florid polysyllables, with juicy sentiments about God, sunsets, the moral improvement inherent in a daily view of mountain scenery, angels, fishing for souls, fishing for fish, ideals, patriotism, democracy. . . . These blossoming words, these organ-like phrases, these profound notions, had been rammed home till they stuck in his brain, ready for use (p. 58).

Thus equipped, Elmer advances to conquer the world. Later he was to learn "that references to Dickens, Victor Hugo, James Whitcomb Riley, Josh Billings, and Michelangelo give a sermon a very toney Chicago air" (p. 116). Though he does not have quixotic benignity, helpfulness, or idealism, he does have visions of how the ministry can be useful to him; he sees "thousands listening to him—invited to banquets and everything. . . ." (p. 62), and he dreams of "hundreds of beautiful women [who weep] with conviction and rush down to clasp his hand" (p. 63).

In addition to his hypocrisy and his ignorance, Elmer is a liar, a sinner, and a coward. Though the bulldog of the football team in college, Elmer shows his cowardice during the fire in Sharon Falconer's tabernacle (which is built out over the water): "In howling panic, Elmer sprang among them, knocked them aside, struck down a girl who stood in his way, yanked open the door, and got through it . . . the last, the only one, to get through it" (p. 225). He then ran out a little into the surf and dragged in a woman who had already safely touched bottom, and then at least thirty more who had already rescued themselves. "A hundred and eleven people died that night, including all the gospel-crew save Elmer" (p. 226).

After the fire and Sharon's death, Elmer is conscience-stricken. He searches for his better nature: he will start again, never lie or cheat or boast. He will begin as a preacher in a small town, will enliven it and lift it. "Life opened before him, clean, joyous, full of the superb chances of a Christian knighthood. Some day he would be a bishop, yes, but even that was nothing compared with the fact that he had won a victory over his lower nature." He kneels in prayer, but in that instant he sees Cleo and at once thinks of seducing her (pp. 265–66).

Elmer, like other Lewis protagonists, fears marriage. After his wedding to Cleo, he gasps to himself, "Oh, good God, I've gone and tied myself up, and I never can have any fun again!" (p. 291). His treatment of her on the wedding night is reminiscent of Eddie Schwirtz's treatment of Una Golden. The bell-boy is scarcely out of the room when Elmer grabs Cleo. She cries out, "Oh, don't! Not now! I'm afraid!" He replies, "That's damned nonsense!" Later he says, "Come on now, Clee, show some spunk!" Making fun of her, he thinks, "Fellow *ought* to be brutal, for her own sake" (p. 293). Brute, fake, or philanderer, Elmer Gantry seems nevertheless destined for a successful career. As he gains experience, Elmer attempts to broaden his mind. He begins a course of home study, in a brief episode which must play ironically against Benjamin Franklin's self-education. Elmer reads Browning, Tennyson, Dickens. To increase his vocabulary he begins a word list: incinerate, Merovingian, Golgotha, Leigh Hunt, defeasance, chanson—romantic-sounding words.

Lewis's ingenuity was not exhausted on Elmer. Sharon Falconer is an equally striking example of his satiric power.[2] She is a monstrous creation who seems to grow in size with each revelation of her craziness. She appears to Elmer as a saint, arms outstretched, stately, slender and tall, passionate.

> Her voice was warm, a little husky, desperately alive.
>
> "Oh, my dear people, my dear people, I am not going to preach tonight—we are all so weary of nagging sermons about being nice and good! I am not going to tell you that you're sinners, for which of us is not a sinner? I am not going to explain the Scriptures. We are all bored by tired old men explaining the Bible through their noses! No! We are going to find the golden Scriptures written in our own hearts, we are going to sing together, laugh together, rejoice together like a gathering of April brooks, rejoice that in us is living the veritable spirit of the Everlasting and Redeeming Christ Jesus!" (p. 157).

Declining from this spirituality, she gives her gospel-crew a pep talk: let's hit people hard for money-pledges. Like ordinary mortals, she is often weary. She is also an insane perversion of the sanctity of the elect, for she declares to Elmer, "I can't sin! I am above sin! I am really and truly sanctified! Whatever I may choose to do, though it might be sin in one unsanctified, with me God will turn it to his glory. I can kiss you like this—" Quickly she touches his cheek, "Yes, or passionately, terribly passionately, and it would only symbolize my complete union with Jesus! I have told you a mystery." She is the supreme fantasist. She has created an enchanted image of herself, and she has convinced her audience of that image, so that they see her as she wants to be seen, and only we, given glimpses of another self when she reveals herself to Elmer, come to know how complete and insane is her transformation. She is of the occult; she is a witch. She tells Elmer that she has visions; God talks to her. But shifting moods again, she can acknowledge that she is just an ignorant young woman with a lot of misdirected energy—and even an evil one: "Oh, I hate the little vices—smoking, swearing, scandal, drinking just enough to be silly. I love the big ones—murder, lust, cruelty, ambition!" (p. 177). She invites Elmer to visit the old Falconer place in Virginia, but when they arrive, she confesses that she is really just Katie Jonas, born in Utica, whose father worked in a brickyard. She had bought the plantation just two years before. "And yet I'm not a liar! I'm not! I *am* Sharon Falconer now! I've made her—by prayer and by having a right to be her!" (p. 184).

That night she seduces him. "Come! It is the call!" He follows her to her bedroom where he sees "a couch high on carven ivory posts, covered with a mandarin coat; unlighted brass lamps in the likeness of mosques and pagodas; gilt papier-mâché armor on the walls; a wide dressing-table with a score of cosmetics in odd Parisian bottles; tall candlesticks, the twisted and flowered candles lighted; and over everything a hint of incense" (p. 185). She gives him a robe for the service of the altar. Like a priestess she takes him to the chapel, a shrine with hangings, a crucifix, statues of the Virgin, and heathen idols, including a naked Venus. Here she kneels. "It is the hour! Blessed Virgin, Mother Hera, Mother Frigga, Mother Ishtar, Mother Isis, dread Mother Astarte of the weaving arms, it is thy priestess. . . ." They read from the Song of Solomon. She sinks into Elmer's arms.

Yet at the fire, it is Sharon who is heroic. "He could hear her wailing, 'Don't be afraid! Go out slowly! . . . Don't be afraid! We're in the temple of the Lord! He won't harm you! I believe! Have faith! I'll lead you safely through the flames!" (pp. 224–25). When Elmer tries to make her escape, she pushes him away. "He looked back and saw her, quite alone, holding up the white wooden cross which had stood by the pulpit, marching steadily forward, a tall figure pale against the screen of flames" (p. 225).

One admirable character, Frank Shallard, makes an essentially quixotic response to Elmer and his deceits. He has been educated by Roger Williams, Adoniram Judson, Luther, Calvin, Jonathan Edwards, George Washington, Lincoln, Robert Ingersoll, William James, and Fraser's *Golden Bough.* "He had learned to assemble Jewish texts, Greek philosophy, and Middle-Western evangelistic anecdotes into a sermon" (pp. 235). Frank's mentor has been Father Pengilly, a fanciful figure whom we have already discussed.

Frank finds some shame in being a preacher and longs to prove that he is nevertheless a "real man." "Not only had he been swathed in theology, but all his experience had been in books instead of the speech of toiling men. He had been a solitary in college, generous but fastidious, jarred by his classmates' belching and sudden laughter" (p. 119). Like Carol Kennicott, he suffers a betrayal by books, for his reasoning had been turned from an examination of men as mammals to the mystic theories of souls and their salvation. Shortly Frank meets more of real life than he is prepared for. In a notable passage Lewis tells us sympathetically of the problems of the rebel, of the preacher or the writer who suffers from sensitivity and innocence:

> He was supposed to cure an affliction called vice. But he had never encountered vice . . . . How long would a drunkard listen to the counsel of one who had never been inside a saloon?
>
> He was supposed to bring peace to mankind. But what did he know of the forces which cause wars, personal or class or national; what of drugs, passion, criminal desire; of capitalism, banking, labor, wages, taxes; international struggles for trade, munition trusts, ambitious soldiers? (p. 234).

Frank suffers from self-consciousness about his occupation; it is the same sense of doubt which Lewis has expressed about the writing career: "Frank still resented it that, as a parson, he was considered not quite virile; that even clever people felt they must treat him with a special manner; that he was barred from knowing the real thoughts and sharing the real desires of normal humanity" (p. 332).

The Reverend McGarry tells Frank simply to accept the church with all its imperfections—with its Gantrys—and turn to giving hope and comfort to the piteous human beings who come to the church for help. But Frank rages on at the inconsistencies in doctrine, the contradictions in the Bible, the evil men who are ministers, and the fools and dullards who work about him in Zenith: Gantry, Bishop Toomis, Chester Brown, Hickenlooper, and Potts—Potts especially, who "gets his idea of human motives out of George Eliot and Margaret Deland, and his ideas of economics out of editorials in the *Advocate,* and his idea as to what he really is accomplishing out of the flattery of his Ladies' Aid!" (p. 373). Frank adds that he doesn't find Jesus an especially admirable character—Jesus was more vain and furious than a leader should be. What of Jesus's teachings? "Did he come to bring peace or more war? He says both. Did he approve earthly monarchies or rebel against them? He says both." Most distressing of all, says Frank, the sermons of the preachers are "agonizingly dull" (pp. 377–78). So Frank leaves the church temporarily to enter the army where he learns to be "common with common men"; he schools himself further with *Ethan Frome, Père Goriot, Tono-Bungay,* and Renan's *Jesus* (p. 382). Later Frank is thrown from the church and he ventures forth as a worker in a charity organization. Traveling in the Southwest, he is beaten and blinded. He calls out to God for help. Afterward, he must resign himself to helplessness for the rest of his life.

Elmer Gantry has been called the "purest Lewis" by Schorer.[3] Form in the novel, he contends, requires that there be an opposition between the individual and society; yet in this book there are "no impediments to Elmer's barbarous rise from country boob to influential preacher." *Elmer Gantry* is a loosely episodic chronicle, he continues, "which suggests at once that there will be no sustained pressure of plot, no primary conflict about which all the action is organized and in which value will achieve a complex definition." At each of the three climaxes in the book, Lewis retreates into melodrama. Thus, Schorer concludes, there is no pressure upon Elmer to be forced into a position of new self-awareness. D. J. Dooley remarks that to Lewis "Christianity is not only untrue, but inconceivable."[4] Dooley feels that *Elmer Gantry* is flawed "because it is neither a realistic portrayal of the state of religion in America nor a caricature whose manifest unfairness can be forgiven because of the wit and humor which have gone into it." True, unless, taking our cue from Sharon Falconer and the multitude of fraudulent evangelistic minor characters in the book, we begin to see *Elmer Gantry* as Lewis's triumphant depiction of a land of demons and grotesques of all sizes and shapes, created from the extremes of human impulse and incapable of self-awareness because they are already beyond it, Elmer included.

Nothing reveals Lewis's isolation from an over-view of life more clearly than the way he dismisses religion. His quest for God is a secular quest. In "A Letter on Religion" published in 1932, Lewis declared: "It is, I think, an error to believe that there is any need of religion to make life seem worth living."[5] He said that he had known several young people who had been reared entirely without thought of churches or of formal theology, and they seemed happy. "Their satisfaction comes from functioning healthily, from physical and mental exercise, whether it be playing tennis or tackling an astronomical problem." While this notion of religious rites on the tennis court is rather curious, Lewis seems nevertheless to acknowledge a religious impulse, even if he would eliminate God and organized churches. Thus Rebecca West could write incisively about the religious and historical perspectives of *Elmer Gantry:* "The passages in the book which present to one what Mr. Lewis regards as the proper attitude to religion are disconcertingly jejune."[6] Miss West goes on to say that like Mark Twain, who in *Connecticut Yankee* looked at medieval Europe and said, "My, weren't they dumb?" Lewis has no sense of the struggle of the human mind to evolve from chaos to the achievements of his age. Miss West points to Frank Shallard's accusation against Jesus: "Did He ever suggest sanitation, which would have saved millions from plagues?" She comments, "As for the suggestion that Christ should have halted on the way to the Cross to recommend the American bathroom, . . . it ought to go into the Americana section of the *American Mercury*." She concludes her essay as follows: "If [Lewis] would sit still so that life could make any deep impression on him, if he would attach himself to the human tradition by occasionally reading a book which would set him a standard of profundity, he could give his genius a chance." Miss West expresses a prevailing attitude toward Lewis, but she does not, I think, understand what his best books accomplished. It may be that the essential lesson which Lewis's experience of America taught him was that the barriers to education, self-discovery, and fulfillment were formidably guarded by exploiters and cranks: thus his anger; thus his satire. His genius took its chance in mockery, parody, grotesquerie, and excessive performance.

Elmer Gantry, then, is notable as the book in which Lewis moved religion to the center of his critique of American values and declared it to have failed. He thereby makes a defiant gesture, nonetheless, somewhat apart from his customary preoccupation with quixotic heroes whom he could admire for their protests, rebellion, and search for freedom.

Chapter 10

Dodsworth

Dodsworth resolves a tension that has resided within Lewis's romantic heroes from the beginning of his career—the tension childishly expressed by Milt Daggett in *Free Air:* "Wonder if a fellow could be a big engineer, you know, build bridges and so on, and still talk about, oh, beautiful things?" For Samuel Dodsworth is another quixotic hero who has taken most of his ideas from romantic novels and booster oratory, who sets out on travels of adventure, and who transforms what he sees by using his fanciful imagination. By the end of the novel, however, Sam will be ready to dismiss much of his quixotism. This action is symbolized principally by his separation from his wife (who herself is a figure of romantic yearnings); but additionally we see it in such a moment as when Edith Cortright (whom Sam has now courted rightly, with common sense and clear vision) influences Sam's designs for a housing development he intends to supervise in Zenith in his new career. Sam's "Sans Souci Gardens" are to consist of imitative houses—"Italian villas and Spanish patios and Tyrolean inns and Tudor manor-houses and Dutch Colonial farmhouses." But Edith advises him otherwise: "Sam! About your suburbs. Something could be done—not just Italian villas and Swiss chalets. . . . Why shouldn't one help to create an authentic and unique American domestic architecture? . . . Create something native. . . . Dismiss the imitation châteaux" (p. 363).

We can sigh with relief. No more châteaux of the kind we have had for Wrenn, Istra, Hawk, Ruth, Milt, Claire, Carol Kennicott, Guy Pollock, and Arrowsmith, as well as for Sam. In this novel both Lewis and his protagonist seem to be working their way free of quixotism. However, we have only to wait for the next novel to see Lewis's old yearnings return.

Dodsworth opens with the language of romance. In a prelude to the story proper, Sam is attending a dance, in a setting called "a sentimental chromo." Young Samuel Dodsworth, like other Lewis heroes before him, sees his idealized girl come to life. He knows at once that "after years of puzzled wonder about the purpose of life, he had found it." It is Fran Voelker, "slim, shining, ash-blonde, her self-possessed voice very cool as she parried the complimentary teasing of half a dozen admirers." Sam is entranced by the sight of Fran. He searches his romantic mind for metaphors for her. He sees himself as a Richard Harding Davis hero; he is "riding a mountain trail, two thousand sheer feet above a steaming valley; sun-helmet and whipcord breeches; tropical rain on a tin-roofed shack" (p. 5). Fran declares that she is grasping; she wants the whole world. Sam promises it to her. She seems a reincarnation of Carol Kennicott, and the connection is established by Fran's "too-gorgeous lounging robe of Chinese brocade," like the costume of the Princess Winky Poo of *Main Street.* Sam's angel is "an angel of ice" (p. 2).

After this prelude the novel skips twenty years of marriage, during which Sam was too busy with his work to be discontented. The story picks up at the point of Sam's retirement from business. He is fifty; Fran is forty-one; the year is 1925. Sam awakens to doubts about his angel; she is too much a manager; she plays at being a kitten, but "she's a greyhound." "She's quicksilver. And quicksilver is hard, when you try to compress it!" Soon enough we are told what Fran can do to her husband: "She had a high art of deflating him, of enfeebling him, with one quick, innocent-sounding phrase. . . . The easy self-confidence which weeks of industrial triumphs had built up in him she could flatten in five seconds. She was, in fact, a genius at planting in him an assurance of his inferiority" (pp. 23–24).

Fran persuades Sam to tour Europe. After twenty years of marriage and with their children grown up, she desires a "new life" before it's too late; she wants to be free. Quickly they sail. And quickly we learn what her new life is to mean: aboard ship "within three days she had a dozen men to 'play with'" (p. 43). Again, Lewis indicates that he no longer admires the young yearner who wishes to play; it is now his Managers and Improvers who play.

Sam's quixotism is fed by books and by travel pictures, which utter magic names: St. Moritz, Cannes, the Grand Canal. He recalls the romanticizing of earlier days, when he would come to the nursery of his daughter Emily and say, "Milord, the Duke of Buckin'um lies wownded [sic] at the gate!" As he and Fran approach Europe he calls forth the inspiration of his wanderlust, Kipling, from whose "The Gipsy Trail" he recites "Follow the Romany patteran."

As the ship nears Britain, Sam feels that "they had fulfilled the adventure, . . . they had come home to England." His imagination is released; he sees and he fancies. We note the images from books that shaped his vision:

> Mother England! Land of his ancestors; land of the only kings who, to an American schoolboy, had been genuine monarchs—Charles I and Henry VIII and Victoria. . . . Land where still, for the never quite matured Sammy Dodsworth, Coeur de Lion went riding, the Noir Faineant went riding, to rescue Ivanhoe, where Oliver Twist still crept through evil alleys, where Falstaff's belly-laugh discommoded the godly, where Uncle Ponderevo puffed and mixed, where Jude wavered by dusk across the moorland, where Old Jolyon sat with quiet eyes, in immortality more enduring than human life (p. 47).

Lewis declares, "Just like in the pictures! England!" Sam's fancy carries him further: "Knights in tourney; Elaine in white samite, mystic, wonderful—no, it was Guinevere who wore the white samite, wasn't it? must read some Tennyson again. Dukes riding out to the Crusades with minstrels playing on—what was it?—rebecks? Banners alive" (p. 66). But, he reflects, "it isn't real! It's fiction! The whole thing, village and people and everything, is an English novel—and I'm in it!" (p. 71).

As with other quixotes, Sam perceives in two steps. First he fancies an image or a story of the object he is confronting; then he is shaken back to reality. For example, we are told that Sam "discovered slowly, and always with a little astonishment, that the French were human. . . ." He asks himself, "Just what did I expect in France? Oh, I don't know. Funny! . . . Guess I thought there wouldn't be any comforts—no bathrooms, and everybody taking red wine and snails for breakfast, . . . and all the men wearing waxed mustaches and funny beards." We are reminded of Carol Kennicott's fantasy of a romantic Frenchman. Sam thinks he should hear Frenchmen say, "Ze hired girl iz vun lofely girl—oo la la—." But of course they say nothing of the kind, and for putting such clichés in his mind, Sam thanks two sources: "They lie so! These speakers at club meetings, and these writers in the magazines!" (pp. 125–26).

The confrontation with reality occurs when he first stereotypes the journalist called Ross Ireland, whom Sam thinks will be shallow-minded, before he comes to understand the "truth" about him: "Sam discovered that Ross Ireland was guilty of reading vast and gloomy volumes of history; that he admired Conrad more than Conan Doyle." This is the Sweeney Fishberg effect, the Oxford Chinese effect. Again, when Sam attends a college reunion he sees Don Binder, "in college a generous drinker, baby-faced and milky, now an Episcopalian rector." Another former classmate was now a major general, "and one—in college the most mouselike of bookworms—was the funniest comedian on Broadway." Once more we hear of the stereotype: "The great traveler of the novelists is tall and hawk-nosed, speaking nine languages, annoying all right-thinking persons by constantly showing drawing-room manners. He has 'been everywhere and done everything.' He has shot lions in Siberia and gophers in Minnesota, and played tennis with the King at Stockholm." But the *real* traveller is actually "a small mussy person in a faded green fuzzy hat, inconspicuous in a corner of the steamer bar" (p. 216). Thus when Sam encounters anyone new, he creates a picture and story of that person, later to be corrected. When he first sees Edith Cortright, who will subsequently be his wife, he thinks: "She's definitely a 'great lady.' Yet I'll bet that at heart she's lonely." We hear echoes of William Wrenn, from the first novel. Soon Edith declares, "I really love housekeeping. I should have stayed in Michigan and married a small-town lawyer." She might be a reformed and contented Carol Kennicott. Sam and Edith see Naples as Carol's vision made real: "The villas along the bay were white and imposing upon the cliff-tops, at the head of sloping canyons filled with vines and mulberries, or, set lower, mediaeval palaces of arcaded and yellowed marble with their foundations in the water" (p. 356).

As Sam views Europe, listens to talk, and thinks, he seems to develop. He plans a change: "He would have a second life; having been Samuel Dodsworth he would go on and miraculously be some one else, more ruthless, less bound, less sentimental. He could be a poet, a governor, an explorer." "He was so tired of dragging out his little soul and worrying over it!" (pp. 340–41).

Dodsworth has been sorely troubled. He knows that his dissatisfaction with America is also a deep dissatisfaction with himself. He asks himself why he had ever gone abroad. "It had unsettled him. . . . How was it that this America, which had been so surely and comfortably in his hand, had slipped away?" (p. 170). Not since *Main Street* and *Babbitt* has a character in Lewis's fiction been so deeply disturbed, so torn among values, so ready for that conflict of person and society which can result in character growth and change.

Lewis believes that such an inner dissatisfaction is not typically European but is peculiarly American. In his crisis Dodsworth, having abandoned business as the foundation of his philosophy, has nothing to put in its place. Religion means nothing to him ("I'd give my left leg if I could believe what the preachers say. Immortality. Serving Jehovah. But I can't. Got to face it alone.") He has a naïve and romantic sense of history—upon his reading that the site of Notre Dame was earlier occupied by a temple of Jupiter, he thinks: "temple of Jupiter. Priests in white robes. Sacrificial bulls with patient wondering eyes, tossing their thick garlanded heads. Chariots. . . The past . . . was suddenly authentic" (p. 141). By being cut off from tradition, he is truly innocent and new, and he must find all things for himself once again. America provides but one cluster of immediate and dramatic definitions of life—success, wealth, and position. It offers no opportunity—no real freedom—for its young people to question the pursuit of happiness and to choose among alternatives.

We should not forget that Fran Dodsworth has her own perception of the defects of America and her own flirtation with European values. She believes that American men do not *like* women enough. They do not provide an ideal worthy of women's sacrifice; certainly the manufacture of motorcars is no ideal. Fran is everywhere entranced by lords and countesses, stately homes, and refined manners. She is drawn into affairs with two examples of European corruption: Arnold Israel, who though an American is in the European—or, as Fran says, "oriental"—tradition of seducers, and Kurt von Obersdorf, who, it turns out, betrays Fran because of subservience to his mother. When the break with Fran comes, Dodsworth celebrates the event with that strange Parisian exotic named Nande Azeredo, who is surely one of Lewis's most striking compounds of fanciful traits. In her, both Lewis and by extension Dodsworth indulge their powers of quixotic enchantment.

Nande has an important role to play in *Dodsworth*, for Sam, the heretofore monogamous hero, spends three days and nights with her as a gesture of his estrangement from his wife. Lewis does not want to provide Dodsworth with a good woman who would divert attention from the crucial affair with Edith Cortright which is yet to come, for the later love is to be mature, platonic, and deep in mutual understanding. Nor can Sam go to a prostitute for one night. So Lewis creates Nande Azeredo. She is a bohemian, an individualist, an amoralist with her own kind of loyal morality. She is described as "a tall, rather handsome girl, with a face as broad between the cheek bones as a Tartar." Approaching Sam, she demands "in an English that sounded as though it were played on a flute, 'Vot's the trouble? You look down in the mout' '" (p. 321). Now follow details that stamp the fantastic upon this portrait of Nande: she is "half Portuguese, half Russian, and altogether French." Numbers mean a lot in building her characterization. At twenty-five, "she had lived in nine countries, been married three times, and once shot a Siberian wolf" (p. 322). Is this not enough? The joke must broaden, even at the cost of stifling the reader's credulity. More exoticism follows: "She had been a chorus girl, a dress mannequin, a masseuse, and now she scratched out a thin living by making wax models for show-window dummies and called herself a sculptress. She boasted that though she had had fifty-seven lovers ('And, my dear, one was a real Prince—well, pretty real'), she had never let one of them give her anything save a few frocks" (p. 322). Along with her exoticism and goodness of heart, Nande knows how to "serve her man," assuring him "that he was large and powerful and real" (p. 322). The result is that "for the first time in his life [Dodsworth] began to learn that he need not be ashamed of the body which God had presumably given him but which Fran had considered rather an error" (p. 323).

Here in her dishevelled flat, amidst dolls, clothes in heaps, and seven canaries, Nande appears to have run away with Sam's good sense and with Lewis's as well. Sam and Lewis together plunge into every fantasy in the repertoire: "What a wife she'd make for a pioneer! She'd chuck this Parisian show like a shot, if she loved somebody. She'd hoe the corn, she'd shoot the Indians, she'd nurse the babies—and if she couldn't get Paris lingerie, she'd probably spin it" (p. 324). Nande could stand as a fabulous figure, but the difficulty is that here she is required for a serious purpose. Lewis wishes the episode to show Sam at a moment of growth in understanding. Instead, we have an author's dream interlude which in another context would be a joke but here distracts from a critical moment in Sam's development.

The last chapters of *Dodsworth* contain, nevertheless, some of the best non-satiric passages Lewis ever wrote—and his best conclusion of a novel. If we are by now prepared to grant Lewis his defects, which seem inevitable, we can see that in *Dodsworth* he keeps them subdued and exploits his strengths. He controls the tone almost completely. He makes clear what Dodsworth is learning from his new companion, Edith Cortright. If the answers to the search are, after all, fairly obvious, they are convincing under the circumstances. The values are embodied in art, in repose, in building and creating, in good talk, and most of all in a sound relationship between persons.

Two passages momentarily disturb the tone. In an ugly phrase he has Edith say something out of keeping with her generous nature: in rejecting New York, she tells Sam that "Russian Jews in London clothes going to Italian restaurants with Greek waiters and African music"—mongrels, she calls them—have contaminated it.[1] In the other passage, we learn that, true to popular fiction and soap operas, the widow Edith Cortright has had an unhappy first marriage. Her late husband was a liar, a drunkard, a brute. Lewis thus gave his hero and lady an occasion for some sentimental sobbing. But he missed the opportunity to dignify Edith by providing her with a mature experience in a happy first marriage.

Nevertheless, all else is well controlled. We are led by a series of comparisons with Fran to understand what Edith stands for: Edith is easy and gay, finds everything in life amusing, keeps her hair long and parted simply "in an age of universal bobbing." Most of all (here we are in the midst of complex attitudes where Lewis is searching once again for just the right balance) she regards painting as neither superior nor inferior to manufacturing (Fran thought it superior): "I neither regard it as inferior, as do your Chambers of Commerce who think that all artists are useless unless they're doing pictures for stocking advertisements, nor do I regard it as superior, as do all the supercilious lady yearners who suppose that a business man with clean nails invariably prefers golf to Beethoven" (p. 336–37). Sam agrees. His own conclusion is that modern businessmen are "about like other people, as assorted as cobblers, labor leaders, Javanese dancers, throat specialists, whalers, minor canons, or asparagus-growers" (p. 337).

Sam finds in Edith sympathy and respect. She is a good cook, she loves housekeeping, swimming, sailing, tennis. In Europe, she says, one can have dignity and privacy. Together they have long, slow, peaceful talks. Sam feels as if he is beginning to change.

So rare is it for Lewis to juxtapose emotions that it is a pleasant surprise to regard the skill with which he cuts across Sam's awakening contentment by means of Fran's shrill-voiced letters. Fran had just written him a long letter ending with shock at the familiarity between her lover the count and his servants; Sam at once thinks of Edith and her kind way with employees. We are told that "in the twilight hush, Edith's voice was quiet, not pricking him with demands for admiration of her cleverness, her singular charms, but assuring him . . . that she was happy to be with him" (p. 358).

In keeping with his ideas about the strength of the pioneers and the influence of the west wind, Lewis gives Edith a speech in which she reveals the message of Europe, the cause of America's failing, and her formula for regeneration through primitivism. Often she lies in her garden, under the hot sun, smelling the earth, finding life (p. 360). Sam responds as she advises; "he turned to the eternal earth, and in the earth he found contentment."

More letters from Fran intrude, in which Dodsworth reads that Fran has been betrayed by her lover. Lewis handles plot and character admirably here. True to his nature, Sam loyally leaves Edith in order to help Fran; true to her nature, Fran is the same, as self-centered and nagging as ever. In a climax in which Sam's growth and change are proved, he returns to Edith, convincingly saddened about his wife, but equally certain that reunion with her would mean little to her and death to his spirit. *Dodsworth* is Lewis's tribute to Europe's values and to America's energy and capacity to learn. So ends the dialectic in Lewis's books. He has evolved a way to fuse, in one man, the thinker and the builder, the sensitive artist and the pragmatic realist. From this point Lewis must seek new attitudes, new perceptions of life, or forever repeat himself. Unfortunately, repetition is what followed.

The problem of investing the eternal doers (as he called Dodsworth and Myron Weagle and Fred Cornplow) with believable heroic qualities was difficult to solve. The rebels and the pariahs like Guy Pollock and Miles Bjornstam of *Main Street* were destined to fail; they do not fail nobly, but pathetically, for Lewis made them weak and intended them to be subordinate to the major figures. Arrowsmith and Dodsworth, however, have some measure of intelligence and dignity, though both have deficiencies as heroes. But some of these deficiencies were intended to indicate that typically American heroes "bumble" and "clump" as well as stride. Whatever Lewis wished to leave to the world as the message of the doers, he left best in *Dodsworth* rather than in any other book.

Professor Grebstein observes that "the critics who have complained that Lewis was incapable of anything but mockery, those who have asserted that Lewis's characters are flat or grotesque, those who deny Lewis any stature beyond that of historian of part of the mood of the 1920's could not have read *Dodsworth*."[2] The book is, in fact, one of Lewis's highest achievements.

His almost indiscriminate ambivalence of attitude toward his characters is shown in his late diary entries. At sixty-one years of age he was still perplexed about those American men whom he had tried to portray during the previous thirty years. He had just spent a long afternoon with "the boys" on a motor-cruiser exploring the Duluth-Superior Harbor. He had been in company with an insurance broker, two bankers, and four real-estate men. They were kindly, touching, lonely. They did charitable work; they told jokes; they belonged to church; they hated Roosevelt and cooperatives. They were kind to an outsider.[3]

These garrulous tellers of dirty stories, these men just marginally honest, these merchants of Zenith—they did the world's building, they could be such good, unselfish fellows. He scorned them, but he *liked* them. Therefore, late in life, Lewis created a new and fond name for them—they were his "Babbittworths."

Chapter 11

The Later Fiction

And so, in 1930, Lewis stood at the podium in Stockholm to receive the Nobel Prize for Literature and to make his response.

He had frankly sought the literary prizes, even though it is sometimes intimated that he was modest and unknowing about them.[1] In the autumn of 1919, after the appearance of *Free Air,* his youthfully optimistic and playful romance of the open road, Lewis wrote to Ellen Eayrs at Harcourt: "Would it be perfectly insane and egotistic to suggest that you or Mr. Spingarn send a copy of the book to the [Pulitzer] prize committee, suggesting that the dern thing is a study in 'the wholesome atmosphere of American life,' etc.?"[2] In 1920 the literary committee for the Pulitzer Prize (Hamlin Garland, Stuart Sherman, and Robert Morss Lovett) chose *Main Street* as the winner, but a reviewing committee rejected it for not portraying these same wholesome aspects of American life. The award went to Edith Wharton instead.

Hearing rumors that *Arrowsmith* might get the prize in 1926, Lewis wrote his publisher that he hoped the committee would nominate the book, but that "ever since the *Main Street* burglary, I have planned that if they ever did award it to me, I would refuse it."[3] *Arrowsmith* was nominated, and Lewis turned the award down. He wrote that he objected to the whole idea of any group reserving for itself the right to choose the best novel of the year.

Lewis's interest in the Nobel Prize also began early. In 1920 he suggested that his publisher should begin pulling the political wires necessary for the highest honors "to see if there may not be one chance in 50,000 that we'd get the Nobel prize on *M St* or a later novel." After all, he wrote, people of influence in the "Ole Country" (he mentions a Mrs. Nohowel) should be shown that *Main Street* is a "picture of Scandinavians in US" (which it is only in part). "I pass this buck to you because I couldn't speak of it to Mrs. Nohowel without seeming egotisticaller 'n hell."[4] In 1925 Lewis was again writing to his publisher, "Any thoughts on pulling wires for *Martin* [*Arrowsmith*] for Nobel prize?"[5] To which Alfred Harcourt replied that he would have Stuart Sherman pull wires in America, while Lewis's publishers in England, Sweden, and Germany would do the same in Europe.[6]

As he approached Stockholm, Lewis might have reflected that he had reached a condition of repose and reconciliation in *Dodsworth.* He had come to an understanding of the glorious playfellows and golden princesses who were a knight's reward, and he had identified the Improving Woman and satirized her, thereby conquering her. Then he had found a comforting and helpful companion for his builders and doers. He had searched for meaningful work for both men and women and had found it. He had evolved a way for a builder to escape dullness and to cultivate an appreciation of beauty. He had exposed frauds, confidence men, wastrels; he had done what he believed Wells had done: exposed the small-minded managers and manipulators who govern the economic, spiritual, and political life of the country. He saw that the task of America was not merely to make and sell things, but to enjoy the countryside and to restore the land. He had written a record of the great American domestic quarrel, and he had defined man, woman, and marriage.

At Stockholm he reviewed the nation's literary history. Then he called upon the future, praising the writing of the young, yet little recognizing how different their work was from his, how much more their work would ultimately be accepted than his own as meeting the requirements of new readers. Now, at forty-six, with a new home and an infant son, he said, "I am settled down to what I hope to be the beginning of a novelist's career."[7] The prize-winner hoped the apprenticeship was over. But through the frankness and realism of the speech we hear with some trepidation a familiar note: "I should have supposed. . . ."; "I should even have supposed. . . ."; "Let me sketch a fantasy . . ."; "I fancy that. . . ."[8]

This would be his fourth beginning. The first had occurred when he started to "scribble"; the second was his discovery of how to use Wells in order to complete *Our Mr. Wrenn;* his third was *Main Street.* But instead of new achievement Lewis's work declined in quality after he received the prize—every critic has noted it, although some have praised several of his later novels. As we review the later fiction, we should note how many of the established quixotic patterns of his work continue to appear.

The novel called *Ann Vickers* is a study of a female quixote. In many ways Lewis retells the story of Una Golden, the protagonist of *The Job*. The setting for much of the action is the same—New York. The themes are similar: finding a career, searching for self-realization as a woman, losing one's innocence, and achieving true love. Though Lewis knew a great deal more about both New York and women than he had known fifteen years earlier, a number of his formulas reappear. Ann, for instance, leaves the small town of Waubanakee, Illinois, with the encouragement of a socialist mentor, Oscar Klebs, who tells her that the capitalist system is wrong. She had read the usual books: *Water Babies*, LeGallienne's *The Quest of the Golden Girl, David Copperfield, Kim, Tono-Bungay;* and as she starts toward experience, she declares, "I want to know." Characterization by ironic surprise also occurs. Ann meets a suffrage leader called Miss Bogardus, the Battle-Axe, who, we are told, "was to the eye and ear the comic journal picture of a suffrage war-horse: a tall, scraggly spinster with ferocious eyes and a loud, shrill, ragged voice." Yet she is not what she seems; "within a fortnight [Ann] had found that Miss Mamie Bogardus . . . was the bravest, the most honest, the kindliest, and the most wistful woman alive." Ann fancies her as "the pioneer grandmother with a baby on one arm and a rifle for the Indians on the other" (pp. 106–108).

Ann possesses qualities which suggest a prototypical feminist. Inevitably, she is a Westerner by birth. She is supposed to have western clarity of thought, western courage, and the pioneering spirit, all virtues which she had learned from her father. She believes in justice, honesty, and fair treatment. At the same time, however, she practices and proselytizes a new creed of behavior which permits free love, abortion, and the sanction of theft when the thief is her lover.

Ann discovers evil in two settings: the prisons and the city. She meets more real horrors than any other Lewis character, and she endures them. In prison there is a hanging and a whipping (such scenes are very vivid), while outside the prison the Common People, the Safe and Sane, remain unaware. Ann is surrounded by temptations, by enemies, by betrayal. Almost everyone is evil or crippled. In New York she is ringed around by pseudo-artists, weakling men, lesbians, homosexuals, and nymphomaniacs. Each man she meets (except one) turns out bad on close examination—Lafe Resnick, who deserts her after making her pregnant; Lindsay Atwell, her indecisive suitor; Russell Spaulding, her degenerate first husband (a sophisticated Eddie Schwirtz). Only Judge Barney Dolphin is big enough to love a Great Woman; that is because he is fabricated from diverse and contradictory materials. He is a scholar, a devotee of wine and wenching, an associate of highly placed politicians. He has a B.A. from Fordham, with a letter in baseball; a Columbia law degree, with a year at the Sorbonne; an honorary L.L.D. He speaks French, Italian, Polish, Yiddish, English, and "East Side"; he is an Elk; he plays billiards and poker; he is an authority on bonds. At fifty-three he can run one hundred yards in thirteen seconds. Although a practicing Catholic, Judge Dolphin has been co-respondent in three divorce suits. He is of mixed heritage: Irish, Cockney, English, Swedish, and Austrian. He drives a cream-colored roadster with low-set red leather seats. He has a wife and two daughters in Europe. He knows when to be silent. And he has taken tips on where the new trolley lines will be built. Thus he knows where to speculate in property. How characteristically Lewis puts forth this confusion of fancy and observation: he still believes the notion that the fanciful accumulation of fact—the exterior appearance of size—will convince his reader that we are dealing with inner complexities. Convicted of misuse of privileged information, Barney Dolphin receives a sentence of six years. But he is pardoned, it appears to me, so that Ann will not have to be deprived of her lover for long. All her experience of evil brings Ann little maturity. As early as page 32 Lewis made a painfully self-revealing estimate of her potentialities for character growth: "Now it is true that Ann Vickers, at fifteen, was all that she would ever be at forty, except for the trimmings."

In *Work of Art* Lewis sets forth the dichotomy of the waster and the doer, like a fable of the idle and the industrious apprentices. He creates two brothers, a hotel manager and a writer, one to symbolize waste, the other creativity. It is significant—and an ironic surprise—that Lewis sees the writer as the wastrel and the hotel man as the creator. The portrait of Ora Weagle, the writer, is spiteful, as if Lewis was engaged upon some revenge against the dreamer, for it may be that he was angry at what he might have been or what his parents feared he would be—lazy and prodigal. There is a furious energy of vindictiveness against Ora, who recapitulates the history and characteristics of the romantic cavalier. We first see Ora dancing on the roof, "a child of the skies." He had read Swinburne, Longfellow, Tennyson, and Kipling. At fifteen he had perceived that he belonged to a world greater than his village, which he despised. He has dreamt quixotic dreams of far-off places—New York, London, Paris, Berlin, Monte Carlo:

> He dreamed—the formless, visual dreams of a young poet: Castles. Girls milk-white. In Xanadu did Kubla Khan a stately pleasure-dome decree. Sleek greyhounds with silver bells. God through unending aeons drowsing on His throne. . . . Wild white horses galloping through the desert, beneath an orange mesa. An archbishop chanting Mass, in vestments stiff with gold. A starving explorer staggering into a Tibetan village. An English cottage among roses. . . . [T]o search in all lands for the Holy Grail. Delectable. Faërie. Clad in white samite, mystic, wonderful. Glamour. Casting down their golden crowns around the glassy sea . . . (pp. 19–20).

He states his ambition: "First I'll do poetry. But what I want to head for is big novels. I expect I'll be the Dickens of America." His career is disorganized, however. He is a hack writer of novels, guides, and filmscripts. He has an affair with an octoroon (one senses that Lewis was dazzled by the exoticism of the word) and declares, "By golly, I'll give the world the first real psychology of the Negro in love and in trouble!" The girl commits suicide and Ora writes his only honest book—or so we are told without learning anything specific about it. Then he returns to hack-writing.

It is Myron, the hotel man, who has the poet's mind. Lewis reverts to his fancies and plays with the unexpected. Myron begins setting down his "Hotel Projects Notes," which, Lewis tells us, "must, in exactness, be called 'The Notebook of a Poet' ": "Most luxurious sanitarium in world, within hundred miles New York, freedom of a hotel, but fine docs, elec equipment, baths, etc. but absolutely quiet, tennis & golf but far enough fr hotel no noise, no dances or music after 10 p.m., but movies nightly? large private balconies where can rest all day" (p. 244). This is poetry only by indulgence. When Myron expresses a philosophy, he does so on behalf of his author, who believes it too:

> What is an art, what is a profession, what is a business, what is a job? Is a man who runs a great grocery store like Park & Tilford, Acker, Charles, or the gr. dept of Macy's just a business man, while anybody who makes smart pictures of girls is artist, and doc or lawyer who thinks about nothing but making money a professional and cranky old prof who goes on handing out same lectures yr after yr a scholar and not just on a white collar job? (p. 254).

Lewis then comments:

> The unfortunate thing is that though men have general resemblances in love, hunger, patriotism, and noses, they differ utterly in the technicalities of their work, and each grieves that all the others are idiots not to understand his particular language. Hotelman or sculptor or sailor or manufacturer of tacks, each has a separate and self-conscious world, with a certainty of its significance to the universe, of the towering dignity of its every detail, and of the fascinating differences between colleagues who, to outsiders, seem indistinguishable "types" (pp. 274–75).

What Lewis was offering in the quoted passages was a serious, forthright statement of ideas and emotions he had held ever since college days. His essay for the *Yale Literary Magazine* called "Unknown Undergraduates" recalls his plea for recognition of the little known student: Remember that all are men "and familiarity with any man, be he only the man who sits next to you in class, or, out of college, merely the waiter, will show that spark which makes him wonderful."[9] Now, in *Work of Art,* a waiter who has risen to the heights of manager of major hotels is the symbol of the worth of all the little men and of the vitality of their humble jobs. This novel ushers in the middle thirties, Lewis's years of such common men as Myron Weagle, Doremus Jessup, and Fred Cornplow.

Clearly, then, with Myron, the "little man" of Lewis's early novels is coming into his own again. In subsequent books his emergence is even more apparent. Doremus Jessup of *It Can't Happen Here* is consciously a portrait of a little man, little in name (his friends call him "dormouse"), in stature, in community position, in mutterings. Nevertheless, Jessup is courageous, scholarly, responsible, and liberal. He is alert to the danger of fascism and communism in the United States. He is willing to fight for democracy and die in the struggle against a homegrown fascist dictatorship. In all respects but one, Jessup upholds conventional moralities.

Jessup's wife Emma is much like Myra Babbitt, dull, plain, good, solid, motherly, but unperceptive, unconcerned, willing to compromise in the fight against fascism. In spite of her goodness, then, Jessup seems justified in finding himself a mate more appropriate to his ideas and his battles. He has no qualms of conscience in taking a mistress. The love between Lorinda Pike and Jessup is pure and idealized, but nevertheless joined to sexual involvement and heightened by excitement growing out of the local and national crisis caused by the overthrow of the American government. Lewis endorses a new morality in his common man, who knows everyone's worth so well as to carve out his own code of morals without hurting anyone. No questions of morality beyond this need be raised. The only point is to see that everyone is happy and no one is hurt. Therefore, Jessup must be careful lest his wife learn that he has a mistress. But it is really Lewis who manipulates events so that she does not know, for many other characters in the book do, and whether it is true to life that Jessup's fascist enemies can know of his affair and not use the information against him is highly questionable.

In effect, Jessup has solved one of the difficulties Lewis often posed for his men. Emma, we are told, is bread, and Lorinda is wine. Thus Jessup gets both types that would make for a man's happiness. The hero declares that "it does all seem so natural."

But if these are the uncomplicated terms of the book's personal relationships, we must not forget that its true target is fascism. The book takes shape from the atrocities that surround and affect the central characters. There are evil figures like Shad Ledue lurking about, and minute men and commissioners who purge and execute in the manner of Nazi Germany. Lewis's fancy also takes advantage of opportunities for heroics, even for the Mati Hari efforts of Jessup's daughter. Yet his contribution to the thirties, when action against decay and depression was advancing all round him, was this: "Pondered Doremus: Blessed be they who are not Patriots and Idealists, and who do not feel they must dash right in and Do Something About It" (p. 138). The book closes with one of the worst sentences to come from the satirist's pen: "And still Doremus goes on in the red sunrise, for a Doremus Jessup can never die."

Eternal doers like Doremus Jessup manage a measure of heroism, in spite of their close relationship to the little men of the early novels. But with Myron Weagle and Fred Cornplow we see Lewis attempting to push the thesis of the value of the common man to its ultimate—by making them not more noble but more commonplace. They are hard workers, loyal in love, ready to serve, and faithful to democracy. But they are not convincingly articulate; their babbitt-talk recalls what Lewis had too often satirized for us to take it very seriously now. And the exposition which surrounds the action offers nothing to sustain heroics or passion.

It is evident from the first chapter of *It Can't Happen Here* that the satiric types are operating in such a context of social and moral danger that our comic responses are stifled. Here we are shown not humbugs but evil men. Those who address the guests on ladies' night at the Rotary Club of Fort Beulah, Vermont (a village which embodies New England democratic and independent virtues), are not simply fatuous this time. No common booster is General Edgeways and no harmless feminist is Mrs. Adelaide Tarr Gimmitch. For though she is made fun of by Lewis for her "Unkies" slogan and "Roundies" nursery rhymes, Lewis is strident in his mockery and explicit in his condemnation of Mrs. Gimmitch's D.A.R.: "The D.A.R. . . . is a somewhat confusing organization. . . . It is composed of females who spend one half their waking hours boasting of being descended from the seditious American colonists of 1776, and the other and more ardent half in attacking all contemporaries who believe in precisely the principles for which those ancestors struggled" (p. 5). Mrs. Gimmitch praises order, saying, "I'm not sure but that we need to be in a real war again, in order to learn Discipline!" (p. 8). Turning to the general, she calls upon him to "'fess up"—instead of talking of peace, let him admit that a war might be a good thing. The general does just that. Some of the things he had said about peace in his earlier speech were not what he really believes; he would tell the world: "Now you boys never mind about the moral side of this. We have power, and power is its own excuse!" He advocates collegiate military-training units "under discipline as rigorous as the Nazis."

This novel continues Lewis's exposure of the hypocrisies of clergymen, here a political preacher, somewhat like Father Coughlin, who had a vast radio audience in the mid-thirties. The Reverend Paul Peter Prang, of Perseopolis, Indiana, delivers a three-page speech, which is too long to quote in full, though some indication of its subject matter and style appears in this excerpt:

> "My friends of the radio audience. . . . For more than a year now, the League of Forgotten Men has warned the politicians, the whole government, that we are sick unto death of being the Dispossessed—and that, at last, we are more than fifty million strong; no whimpering horde . . . we have demanded . . . that International Jewish Finance and, equally, International Jewish Communism and Anarchism and Atheism be, with all the stern solemnity and rigid inflexibility this great nation can show, barred from all activity . . . How long now, O Lord, how long. . . ?" (pp. 51–53).

The presidential candidate of the fascists is Senator Berzelius Windrip. "Buzz" Windrip, Lewis tells us, "was almost a dwarf, yet with an enormous head, a bloodhound head, of huge ears, pendulous cheeks, mournful eyes" (p. 85). Windrip was "vulgar, almost illiterate, a public liar easily detected, and in his 'ideas' almost idiotic, while his celebrated piety was that of a traveling salesman for church furniture, and his yet more celebrated humor the sly cynicism of a country store." He was a "Professional Common Man" (pp. 86, 87). Under the spell of Windrip's "orgasms of oratory" you thought he was Plato, though you couldn't later remember anything he had said. In his speech Windrip would slide from the humility of the greenhorn "into a rhapsody of general ideas—a mishmash of polite regards to Justice, Freedom, Equality, Order, Prosperity, Patriotism, and any number of other noble but slippery abstractions" (p. 119). The formula for booster-speeches has become a method of political campaigning. Lewis continues: "Something in the intensity with which Windrip looked at his audience, looked at all of them, his glance slowly taking them in from the highest-perched seat to the nearest, convinced them that he was . . . telling them the truths, the imperious and dangerous facts, that had been hidden from them" (p. 119). Even Doremus Jessup must admit, "I'll be hanged! Why he's a darn good sort when you come to meet him! And warm-hearted. . . . What if Buzz is right?"

Buzz remains a man of simple tastes even after having served as President in a regime which brings Nazi-like rule to America. Here Lewis reiterates his abiding conviction that his babbitts and charlatans are basically "good fellows." Of Buzz, he writes, "He was a sensible man, who preferred straight bourbon, codfish cakes, and deep leather chairs" (p. 415). When Lee Sarason takes over the dictatorship, the appeal of Buzz's good simple nature is so strong that instead of being killed he is exiled to Paris where "he was profoundly homesick for Chesterfield cigarettes, flapjacks, Moon Mullins, and the sound of some real human being saying 'Yuh, what's bitin' you?' " I am reminded of Lewis's remark in the *Nation* in 1928:

> Actually I like the Babbitts, the Dr. Pickerbaughs, the Will Kennicotts, and even the Elmer Gantrys rather better than any one else on earth. They are good fellows. They laugh—really laugh. I have for them only three Utopian ideals: that they should know a little more about history; that they should better comprehend the difference between Irish stew in America and fried mushrooms at Schoener's in Vienna; and that they should talk of the quest of God oftener than of the quest for the best carburetor.[10]

In 1928 there was little reason to take such a statement seriously. It embodies a familiar formula of Lewis's. It comes from his desire to tease and outrage his listeners, his interviewers, and his readers. Many of his characterizations are made up of simple opposites. If you expect the worst of such fellows, you'll find it, but they can be good fellows, too—that is the surprise. When Lewis puts Gantry into the list, one protests more. Lewis has taught us to think Gantry malicious and cowardly, and has rarely shown him to be a good fellow. Elmer violates half of the Ten Commandments. But concerning Buzz Windrip we must expect something more perceptive from Lewis. Lewis ought not to joke with us in all cases.

Buzz is an American Nazi, and Lewis, to his credit, had taken the trouble as early as 1935 to show his readers Nazism in America. Therefore we must insist that Buzz is one charlatan for whom the epithet "good fellow" can bring no sympathy from us. Are we to forget the murders of the Windrip regime? Are we to concede to Lewis that a Hitler-like dictator can be merely a nice guy?

We can grant Lewis his affection for the babbitts. If he chose also to diffuse the effect of his novels by issuing contradictory utterances in interviews, we at any rate still have the novels, themselves, as the more crucial statements of his perceptions. In some novels the anger is unalloyed. In some it is tempered with understanding and pity—though too rarely. But we can ask him to limit his foolery. If he insists upon a view of human nature that allows any contradiction for the sake of a joke, Lewis cannot touch us with a final sense of tragedy.

In the mid-thirties, with communism and fascism rampant, Lewis finds qualities in his babbitts that he can admire, and Fred Cornplow, of *The Prodigal Parents*, becomes a hero. In some ways Cornplow is a reincarnation of William Wrenn. He, for instance, consults a travel agent, who sells "the mist of dawn over rosy seas, Norman cathedrals, goat-loud uplands in the Massif Central," and from whose office Fred leaves with pamphlets on "Why Not Winter in Flowery South Africa, Native Dances in the Island of Celebes, and Ski Haunts in the Tyrol" (p. 98). Fred will fulfill these dreams when he retires from business a year hence. Lewis moves toward the apotheosis of Cornplow (and thus of Babbitt): "For who in the world has ever been more important than Fred Cornplow? He has, at times, been too noisy or too prosy; he has now and then thought more of money than of virtue and music; but he has been the eternal doer." He is the man of the middle class, "equally depended upon—and equally hated—by the savage mob and by the insolent nobility"

(p. 99). "When Fred Cornplow was an Egyptian, it was he who planned the pyramids, conciliated the mad pharaohs, tried to make existence endurable for the sweating slaves. In the days when he was called a Roman Citizen, he was a centurion and he conquered Syria and ruled his small corner of it with as much justice as the day allowed." At one point in history, he was Fr. Abbot Cornplow; at another he was a captain under Cromwell; as Private Fred Cornplow of Massachusetts and Private Ed Cornplow of Alabama, he fought the Civil War. From his family came "nearly all the medical researchers, the discoverers of better varieties of wheat, the poets, the builders, the singers, the captains of great ships. Sometimes his name has been pronounced Babbitt; sometimes it has been called Ben Franklin." Lewis concludes this tribute: "He is the eternal bourgeois, the bourjoyce, the burgher, the Middle Class, whom the Bolsheviks hate and imitate, whom the English love and deprecate, and who is most of the population worth considering in France and Germany and these United States. He is Fred Cornplow; and when he changes his mind, that crisis is weightier than Waterloo or Thermopylae" (pp. 99–100).

The thirties were a puzzling and troubled period. To meet the crises of the decade Lewis elevated Fred Cornplow to the position of savior. Cornplow's children, in fact, are the new danger; they are self-indulgent; they flirt with communism. Lewis counselled energy, excitement, and the medieval quest as the proper attitude for the times. But *Bethel Merriday*, which, because of his long-standing interest in the theater, may have been an inevitable novel, is an escape from public conflicts into private trivialities. Bethel herself is merely a name; no one in the book comes "alive" in any sense. The challenging decade was over.

In the 1940s Lewis found the impetus to write a book that, if not so good as his work of the twenties, is at least better than that of the thirties: *Cass Timberlane*. But first, in *Gideon Planish*, he enlisted a "subject"—education and the philanthropic organizations—and plotted a clash between the charlatan and the Improver, a confrontation he had not tried before. The novel begins in amusement and ends in bitterness. At first, the man whom Peony Planish manipulates does not really mind what she does. He is an ambitious charlatan and he sees that she is better at planning a career than he is. She seduces him, plans the wedding, and outlines his career. As a professor of literature at Kinnikinick College, Gideon believes that teaching should be manly and practical. It is Peony who gets him a deanship by cultivating the right people and by spreading lies. Step by step, Lewis shows us how an Improver, working on willing material, shapes a career.

But Gideon wakes up because of a "Mr. Johnson," who is Lewis's common man, eternal doer, Everyman—from the Midwest: the newspaperman, farmer, small merchant, labor-union secretary, millionaire lumberman (so runs the list). Mr. Johnson discovers that Gideon's organization is taking money, making a fuss, but accomplishing nothing. World War II has begun, and Mr. Johnson *does* something; he joins the Navy. "Suddenly, a little heavily, [Gideon] liked Mr. Johnson of Minneapolis, and agreed with him against all the organizators and all the ethical raptures of his transmogrified Peony" (p. 412). Johnson is a vague instrument of change, perhaps, but Planish responds anyhow. The chance to return to Kinnikinick College as president is a relief to him; he feels reborn. On a trip to Iowa he realizes that his heart resides in the Midwest. But by now his wife controls him. She can make him stay in New York. The last we see of Planish, he is a beaten man, servant to his wife, the Arranger and Improver.

Cass Timberlane is not a satire of a profession, but the story of a marriage between a man of forty and a woman of twenty-five. It dramatizes distressing personal relationships again, and gives us the closest return we have to Lewis's best work of the twenties. Cass, a judge in a city of eighty thousand called Grand Republic, Minnesota, is one of Lewis's competent men, seeking what he calls the Quiet Mind, a life of stability and comfort. He is a quixote. Though he is not addicted to travel, he is much given to enchantment and in his role as judge will set wrongs aright. He lives a lonely life in a community of trivial conversations, racial and economic inequities, and a dozen fitful marriages among his friends. We learn that his first wife, Blanche, had been much like Fran Dodsworth, dreaming of excitement. She encouraged Cass to run for Congress, and in Washington she entertained freely and loved it "like a drunkard." But Cass longed for the quiet of the Midwest and refused to run for re-election. Blanche rebelled and divorced him. As the book opens, the judge is thinking of marriage once more. The choice is between two women: Jinny Marshland, "a half-tamed hawk of a girl, twenty-three or -four, not tall, smiling, lively of eye," with "something daring in her delicate Roman nose, her fierce black hair" (p. 4); and

Christabel Grau, "a plump and rather sweet spinster of thirty-two" (p. 21), "a round and soft and taffy-colored virgin with strands of gray" (p. 25). The half-tamed hawk descends from the princesses—lively, daring, but neurotic, ambitious, pretentious, and selfish. In some ways she resembles Blanche, whom Cass had married and divorced; Lewis's heroes are destined to repeat their errors. On the other hand, the plump and taffy-colored spinster probably would bring great comfort, but not enough excitement. Lewis states the comparison between the two girls in a commonplace metaphor: "If Jinny Marshland was like Cleo, a thin and restless and exciting young cat, Chris was the serene tabby cuddled and humming on the hearth" (p. 25). Jinny (like a more recent Carol Kennicott) first turns to the little theater, then to New York City, which she finds dull when she is with Cass but exciting when with Bradd Criley. She announces to Cass that she loves Bradd and must live in New York. It appears that Cass will have a bleak winter on the prairies.

However, the affair in New York does not go well. Soon Jinny is very sick, and she sends for long-suffering Cass. As in a soap opera, she is in a coma when he arrives. He pushes people out of the way and stalks into the sickroom. The doctor tells him she can recover only if she has the will to live. Cass offers forgiveness. She replies with superficial guilt and shallow self-recognition: "I *have* been a fool! I was young—but not that young! I do know a little better now. Quicksilver people like Bradd slide away from you so. Take me away from here, Cass, please do!" (p. 380). If all this seems like a romantic dream-wish of the author—it is. The novel ends as he wants it to end, with the solid virtues of middle-age asserted, and with forgiveness for the wandering young lady if only she will come home. The mature men are best, and the quiet life is justified. The East is to blame. "I guess that after being lost in these Eastern crowds, so indifferent, I want to go some place where they love you enough to hate you if you don't love *them*" (p. 383). Cass nods, and the tone of the ending suggests that Lewis assents, too. Though scattered throughout the book are many effective sketches of unhappy marriages, at the end of *Cass Timberlane* we have come to another moment of reconciliation and repose in Lewis's work. A protagonist has both his vocation and his helpmate.

Among Lewis's last quixotes is Neil Kingsblood of *Kingsblood Royal*. He is intended to be a typical young American of the years after the second World War: "red-headed, curly-headed, blue-eyed, stalwart, cheerful, and as free of scholarship as he was of malice" (p. 7). When his researches into the family history reveal that he has a small fraction of Negro blood, he announces that fact to the community of Grand Republic, Minnesota, and challenges its racial prejudices. There are some men, Lewis said in reply to an inquiry as to why Kingsblood did not keep this circumstance a secret, who are so honest that they must involve themselves in moral issues no matter what the consequences.[11] In this respect, Kingsblood must be thought of as the noblest of Lewis's heroes. Here, toward the close of his career, Lewis still thought of his heroes in quixotic terms: Kingsblood, he went on to say, fought "with a grimness and a valor probably greater than that of any fancy medieval knight." In many sketches in the book Lewis cuts to the heart of prejudiced whites, though he wavers between effective portraits of blacks and portraits based only on the surprise we feel as we see opposites of what the stereotypes usually indicate. However, such melodrama surrounds the story (including a stand at the barricades in the final chapter) that the moral is somewhat weakened.

With the final two books of his career, Lewis's skill fell away disastrously. Here all the old patterns and tricks are used again, but the imagination and energy have failed. What we see are Lewis's ideas embarrassingly naked and weak. Nonetheless, *The God-Seeker* is interesting because it provides portraits of the pioneering ancestors of Lewis's modern adventurers. His next-to-last book, it is written as if to provide background and justification for his whole vision of contemporary characters.

Selene Lenark, daughter of Caesar Lenark, a fur-trader who lives at a missionary outpost in the Minnesota Territory, is an Indian princess. Selene tells Aaron Gadd of her Indian blood, adding, "There's some Dakota warriors like knights—in *Ivanhoe*." (Are these the lost knights of Minnesota?) Aaron reacts as a hero of Lewis's weaker novels must: he "kissed her as tenderly as though she were his sister."

Aaron had ridden west from Massachusetts in 1848 to become a missionary, asserting his sense of destiny as Carl Ericson might: "Never since the Puritans came to Boston and highmindedly turned a wilderness into a prison . . . had there been such a chance in history as this opening of the North Middlewest" (p. 99). Other passages repeat Lewis's controlling attitudes. For instance, in one place Lewis goes out of his way to offer a lesson in realism. He denies the picture of St. Paul, Minnesota, given in romantic fiction: the brave Catholic padres, gold-laced soldiers, bright-eyed ladies with silk parasols, statuesque Sioux chiefs. No, the real St. Paul was quite different, he says. The symbol of the city in 1850 is a drunken Indian who says to Aaron, with what Lewis calls the universal whine of the beggar, "Gimme two bits, Mister. Hungry!" (pp. 101–102). But strangely, Lewis's "real" Indian seems to talk like a modern babbitt; he brings back to mind the Oxford Chinese butler who awaited Lewis behind the San Francisco hotel door—all paradoxical romantic fantasies of a kind peculiar to Lewis.

When Selene reenters the novel more than a hundred pages after she and Aaron have parted, she has New York ways, which she, like Ruth Winslow and Claire Boltwood, will have to cast out. Expelled from her father's house, she goes to Aaron for comfort; they cling together "like terrified children." They escape, boy and girl together on the prairie (pp. 326–37). A blizzard arises. "Oh, we *are* lost children!" they exclaim. Selene cries, "My brother Aaron, my only brother. . . . I love you." When all hope is lost, they are saved by Huldah Purdick. Aaron notes that Huldah is "a real woman, . . . and Selene is a baby." But like his spiritual descendant Cass Timberlane, he chooses to marry the baby.

Furthermore, the Reverend Harge talks like a forefather of the babbitts. For example, he says to Black Wolf, the Indian educated at Oberlin College, "Blackie, how'd you like to be a teacher for us? Mighty hard to get the spondulics out of the Board, but guess I could fix it to pay you handsome, maybe twenty-five a month" (p. 193). Then Black Wolf, talking better English on each succeeding page and becoming both more learned and more suspect (in the Sweeney Fishberg manner), introduces Aaron to his mother. All people in all ages are somehow alike, and Medicine Spider, we are told, "was the true Mother in Zion, the female pillar of the Protestant Church," such as Aaron had known in New England, at church services and suppers (p. 210).

As a result of various disillusionments, Aaron Gadd becomes that other kind of god-seeker whom we have come to expect in Lewis. Leaving missionary work, he vows to seek God in secular life, as all Lewis heroes must. When Aaron and Selene marry, there is no time for a honeymoon; they merely take a walk. "They did not talk very much; but in his 'This is awful nice—I'm glad we got it together' were all the songs since Solomon," says Lewis (p. 351). No—one is tempted to reply—not any of the songs. Such a remark was Lewis's special effort to make his books timeless, but it is a notable failure. His characters often have nothing graceful to say at crucial moments; some utter romantic clichés; some remain silent. To sustain interest at the end, Lewis falls back on one of his virtuoso performances by introducing Dr. Alfred Munce of the gospel of Synthesism, a charlatan who can be made to speak a satirical set-piece. Then the novel ends quietly with Aaron bringing labor harmony to Minnesota and helping prepare the way for populism.

Lewis's final novel returns to the present and the agony of personal relationships. In *World So Wide,* Hayden Chart, thirty-five years old and recently widowed of a nagging wife, asks himself the fundamental question, "Is this all I'm going to get from life? I've done so little and seen so little." He then seeks the larger, more significant values in Florence, Italy. There he overcomes the temptations of an Arranger and the villainy of Lorenzo Lundsgard, a fraudulent professor, before he finds a princess who will go with him to Burma, Brazil, Damascus.

Although I have found the weak novels of Lewis's last years to be aids in the understanding of his work as a whole, I do not wish to close with an emphasis on them that diverts attention from a consideration of his important and permanent work. These books were written at the tag-end of his days. According to Frederick F. Manfred, Lewis knew that he had for the most part lost his powers. It is a sad account that Manfred gives of what Lewis told him in 1942; Lewis said:

> That's the way it goes. For a little while you have it. The old bite, the old sting. And you give it to 'em while you have it. And everybody cheers and everybody says, "He's really on today, isn't he? He's really hot this time! Wow!" But it isn't long before it's all gone. The vim, the vigor, the celestial spark. All gone. . . . You may kid yourself for a little while that you've still got it, of course. . . . But after a while, when none of the stung die, it becomes apparent it was a hollow show.[12]

I have quoted from the last novels to indicate what the old themes were, what the habits were, the weaknesses, the standard character types, the ideas when reproduced without imagination. Missing from these books is the excitement the creator conveys when he is making discoveries, when he is finding fresh materials and new insights rather than reproducing old ones. Also gone is the sense of fresh language and of characters revealed for the first time. Thus Chart is simply a variation on Dodsworth, whereas Dodsworth himself evolved painfully. Chart's eager playing with the foolish, shallow, and selfish Olivia Lomond (who is herself given an unbelievable history in contrast to Fran's credible one) cannot compare to Sam's loyalty to his wife. The voice of the Reverend Munce, at the end of *The God-Seeker,* is no longer a revelation.

Using these materials over again, Lewis could not invest them with new meanings. There was a cycle in Lewis's work; his last books contain the same materials as his earliest, in much the same spirit—the same romance, the same obvious dichotomy of women, the same baby-talk and play, even the same targets for satire. As he worked with these materials during the apprentice years, Lewis came to understand them. After 1920 he revolted enough against the sentimental romance to keep it pretty much in check. He saw play as foolish and ascribed eagerness for play to foolish women. He mastered the babbitt-voice, learning to alter it according to different manifestations at various economic levels and in various professions. He saw deeper into the yearnings of his men. He distinguished more clearly between those deserving satire and those worthy of pity or admiration. Thus he was able to write his best books during one decade of extravagance and hard work.

Chapter 12

Conclusion

Let us return to Carol Kennicott of *Main Street,* who is so central to Lewis's work that we have discussed her character and plight several times already. Let us consider the problem of "Winky Poo"—that is, the question as to whether Lewis saw, at the time he was writing, the foolishness of Carol's standards of art and reform, as exemplified in the party she holds for her friends at which she asks them to costume themselves in Chinese hats and she appears before them in an Oriental robe, exclaiming, "The Princess Winky Poo salutes her court!" (p. 78). Looking at "Main Street's Been Paved" in the *Nation* four years after publication of the novel, we can see that Lewis made Carol the victim of his own changing attitudes. But *she* is frozen forever in her book, doomed to reenact her life at any reader's cue, exposing her misjudgments, while Lewis moves on in insight. When he conceived of her, he and she looked out upon the world from very nearly the same point of view, side by side. Her way of looking—through Arcady and the Yang-tse—was still his own, and her Chinese costume was an objectification of her quixotic vision, an objectification she thought innocent enough. I think Lewis at first believed it to be harmless, too; her Chinese party need not be a model of all parties, but it was a harmless indulgence of a fanciful interest, and, beyond that, a plausible escape from Gopher Prairie. Arcady and the Yang-tse were ways of enchanting the village scene, transforming it from liver-colored clapboards and bloodreeking meat-store windows to something imaginatively engaging, and of making connections between "home" and the exotic "elsewhere" of older times, far-off places, and her literary heritage. He was gathering hints that Carol's view was foolish. Later he became convinced that it was so. Then he placed her at a distance from himself, as he had done often before with cults and fads.

The fanciful vision, which dominates each protagonist through

Arrowsmith, remains present, is a problem, and becomes a source of nostalgic sympathy in later heroes, especially in Dodsworth and Cass Timberlane. What one discovers is that the fanciful vision has been shifted, for the most part, away from the heroes, so that no later hero quite has it entirely. For instance, it was shifted, in bitterness yet therapeutically, I think, to Ora Weagle, a figure of contempt, and then to innumerable minor characters. Nonetheless, some element of fancy invariably remains throughout Lewis's work. Thus, in *Ann Vickers* it appears in Ann's fantasies about her aborted child, whom she calls "Pride," in the man who seduces her, who must be that out-moded villain the New York Jew, and in her lover Judge Dolphin, who is so big as to be above the law. It is also present in *Dodsworth* in a figure like Nande or in *Timberlane* and *Kingsblood* in Sweeney Fishberg.

Lewis attempted to convert to good use the quixotic impulses he had by making fanciful ascriptions the method of creating largeness of character; the extremes, in fact the contradictions, of behavior led to the "fabulous" figures that Constance Rourke saw in Lewis's books and appropriately named. Lewis converted his fancy to Münchausen-like ends—to tall tales—which thereby gave his people "folkloristic" or "mythic" features. We have noted that Perry Miller thought Lewis "in love with mythological and typological creations like Micawber and Gradgrind." By "mythic" I suggest that Lewis casts over his characters an aura of knighthood and medieval romance and sets them forth on a quest, for example, and by "folkloristic" I suggest that he connects his types to American pioneers, to confidence men, to orators and braggarts. Occasionally he gives a character (like Hawk Ericson, Arrowsmith, Kingsblood, or Aaron Gadd, for instance) such elements of the traditional hero as uncertain parentage, a mentor, a shadowy co-worker, a period of wandering, and a final withdrawal from society. In a way that one can only admire for its audacity, Lewis even measures Dodsworth and Cornplow against his own archetypal creation called "Babbitt" (whose name *had* entered the lexicon, after all)—Dodsworth was *not* a babbitt, we are told, though Cornplow had been a babbitt throughout all history.

A lot of Lewis's flamboyant maneuvering is a substitute for style and thought. The novels do not show evidence that Lewis worried over the full implications of "style," though as a parodist he was attentive to corruptions of language. Corruptions of language correspond to the corruptions of society, and Lewis can be said to have followed Cervantes and Mark Twain in his effort to expunge such evil.

Although Wells, Lewis's mentor, expended effort and wordage on argument, it was Wells's early, less didactic books that Lewis liked. From these Lewis did pick up some ideas about progress, socialism, ethics, and religion, which he made use of. But these ideas have a quixotic naïveté about them as they are enunciated by Professor Fraser, or by Hawk Ericson, or by Gottlieb, Arrowsmith, Dodsworth, Ann Vickers, and Cass Timberlane. One thing Lewis does when he wishes to make use of "ideas" is to satirize the stupidity of a character who has garbled them.

Still, what Wells did for Lewis in 1910 to 1915 Lewis needed to have done again for him after 1930—that is, he needed a stimulus; he especially needed new ways of seeing and conceptualizing. He approached the ensuing years, however, by further exploiting his satire and his character types. Through the influence of Dorothy Thompson, his sense of justice was stirred. He attacked prisons in *Ann Vickers*, although prisons were not the central problem of the time. He attacked native fascism and communism in *It Can't Happen Here* and *The Prodigal Parents;* in both books, however, he blunted his attacks by employing gross cleverness and using as protagonists his "little men." He turned from the excesses of the right and left, but he did so in the name of nothing which would enrich his own work. One might desire some better motive for social criticism than the motive he gives to an unidentified young man in *Gideon Planish* who has been listening to a power-hungry propagandist who "attacked Fascism so hysterically, and with such a suggestion that he was the one lone anti-Hitler, that I almost found myself beginning to be pro-Fascist, anti-Semite, anti-Chinese, anti-feminist, anti-socialized-medicine, anti everything I had always believed in" (p. 423). Because one perceives the foolishness in an advocate of one point of view one need not run to the opposite extreme. To do so was characteristic of Lewis, however. It is the perverse attitude of the village atheist, of the bad boy of letters, of the quixote, yet it has done Lewis the disservice of drawing from some critics the charge that he had no standards, that he cannot imagine any protagonist capable of a sustained struggle, and that he created no truly individual character to resist social types, though Carol Kennicott, Sam Dodsworth, and Cass Timberlane belie that judgment.

A sense of life as tragic might have enabled him to surmount uncertainties and inconsistencies by looking above the characters in some overall view of human nature; he might have moved beyond 1930, the year of the prize, toward new achievements. But Lewis did not have such a view, and if my interpretation of Lewis's career is correct, it was the thin air of the culture at the turn of the century and the temptations and illusions of fancies and cults which deprived him of it. He freed himself in part from these, but they returned to weaken his later work.

He lacked a framework for belief, whether it be humanism, socialism, modern psychology, or religion. Of course, to have been a doctrinaire socialist, for example, would have been an error for him, yet Lewis's ideas on politics or economy were ill-defined. Perhaps with a remark about a minor figure, Mamie Magen, in his third novel, *The Job,* he came closest to stating what his social goal was—the advent of a "scientific era": "Mamie Magen was a socialist who believed that the capitalists with their profit-sharing and search for improved methods of production were as sincere in desiring the scientific era as were the most burning socialists" (pp. 181–182). Such a statement muddles definitions and illuminates little; yet it is so warmly attributed to an admired character as to suggest that the author agrees. In the same manner, late in life Lewis told an interviewer that he felt that the United States was still moving toward socialism (he instanced the post office), that the best socialism was that of the Social Democrats of Germany, and that he would like to vote for Senator Arthur Vandenburg for President.[1]

One will always remember a number of effective scenes in Lewis's books: Carol walking down Main Street for the first time; the episodes during Babbitt's day—at the breakfast table, in the office, at the club; the parties in *Main Street* and in *Babbitt*; Babbitt's speech before the Real Estate Board; Vergil Gunch and his friends stalking Babbitt during his rebellion: Paul and Zilla Riesling quarreling; the petty Tozers of Wheatsylvania in *Arrowsmith*; the visit to Pickerbaugh's family; Gottlieb's sad defeats; the beating of Frank Shallard; Elmer Gantry's hollow triumph; Dodsworth's lonely clumping from place to place; the prisons in *Ann Vickers*. Lewis's novels get their shape from a patterning of characters along a biographical storyline: the hero, his mentor or friend, the rebel, the gallery of portraits of the professional circle, the choices between at least two kinds of women, and the regular reappearance of Lewis's satiric virtuoso orators.

Beyond the brilliance of satire, there should be aspects of characterization which suggest deeper meanings. Lewis certainly intended these, as his preoccupation with the idea of the God-seeker would indicate ("the quest of scientists after God" in *Arrowsmith,* the God-seeking motive behind the proposed labor novel, *Neighbor,* and even the notion that Myron Weagle serves God through humane management of an inn). Furthermore, Lewis's insistence that he was interested in both the typicality and the individuality of his characters and locales suggests that he was trying to understand and explain America in breadth and in detail. Yet it must be acknowledged that Lewis's quixotic heroes show a weakness of ultimate definition that prevents them from evoking the admiration that we have for Gavin Stevens, let us say, in Faulkner's *The Town* and *The Mansion.*

Lewis pictured an America of false beliefs and of material strength. The men who created material America could be justifiably proud of their achievement, yet they might well yearn for an enrichment in their lives which could come with a larger sense of purpose, if only they didn't consider economics the sole motivation and end of their work. Thus in Lewis the American hero would be a fusion of the builder and the man of culture, who does his job and pays his debts responsibly, yet reads, views art, discusses ideas. The western wind blowing clear for him may clean away corruption, dullness, and bewilderment.

In his portraiture, Lewis exposed the failings of the babbitts, men of small spirit who all too sadly seemed to him to be the most characteristic of Americans. More than them, however, he hated fakers and pretenders: bohemian wasters, trivial sophisticates of the city, and charlatans in education, art, religion, and government. He directed his satire against domineering women, but he sympathized deeply with exploited women who rebel against enslavement at home or in menial jobs. He cried out against poverty, prejudice, materialism, and shallow education. He was outraged by stupidity. He felt that the cause of the world's troubles was lack of the use of reason; on the contrary, the use of reason could cure the world. He could build quite a powerful outrage against injustices, and this outrage animated his best scenes. Therein many of his people suffer memorably.

Lewis accomplished a great deal in his writing career. As America's first Nobel Prize winner in literature, he became for Europe the symbol of America's coming of age. He was a leader on best-seller lists in the United States; he was a spokesman in quarrels with the Old Gang; he helped destroy one picture of the small town and substitute another; he attacked various abuses; his name was better known by the general public than that of any other writer in the twenties, when his rejection of the Pulitzer Prize, the reception of *Elmer Gantry*, and the Nobel Award caused sensations, as the *New York Times* for those years testifies. He had many champions who have called him the finest writer of his time. If that judgment goes too far, yet it must be recognized that he worked notably toward portraying an America in which values of trust and honor might be understood more clearly.

Something of the complex reaction many readers feel toward Lewis the quixote and his quixotic novels can be seen by looking at the opposing ways in which Ernest Hemingway and Thomas Wolfe reacted to him and portrayed him in their fiction.

For Hemingway Lewis acted (and wrote) in bad taste, in violation of Hemingway's strict code of behavior in regard to drink, women, and the craft of writing. In *The Sun Also Rises* Hemingway, we recall, had cast the quixotic figure Robert Cohn out of his society in disgrace. Later he had had Frederick Henry, in *A Farewell to Arms*, declare his disillusionment with quixotic abstract words such as glory, honor, and courage. Innumerable Hemingway tyros must learn the code, and the code is surely anti-quixotic (that is, not romantic, sentimental, or illusory).

What became a vituperative exchange with Hemingway opened with Lewis's laudatory remarks in the Nobel Prize speech of 1930: "There is Ernest Hemingway, a bitter youth, educated by the most intense experience, disciplined by his own high standards, an authentic artist whose home is in the whole of life."[2] But in Hemingway's *Green Hills of Africa*, published just a few years after the Nobel Award to Lewis, Kandisky asks, "Who is the greatest writer in America?" and is allowed to add, without contradiction from Hemingway, "Certainly not Sinclair Lewis."[3] Lewis answered with a parody of *Green Hills* in the *Saturday Review:*

> The kudu was a good 470 metres away. I grabbed up my Mannlicher, muttering to the Laconic Limey, "Thoreau is lousy—Willa Cather is a bum—Josephine Johnson is an illiterate brat." I threw down the Mannlicher and grabbed up my Sharps's. . . .

"Santayana is lousy. He never slaughters any animals. None at all. Thornton Wilder is terrible. So was Emerson," I said.

The kudu stopped and died. We all had a drink of beer. We felt fine.[4]

In his review of *To Have and Have Not,* Lewis said that this "alleged novel" demonstrates that "all excellently educated men and women are boresome and cowardly degenerates, while unlettered men engaged in rum running and the importation of Chinese coolies are wise and good and attractive." He called the book dull, and said that it "continues logically the combination of puerile slaughter with senile weariness which was betrayed a couple of years ago in his hunting chronicle 'The Green Hills of Africa.'" Then Lewis concluded, "Please, Ernest! You could have been the greatest novelist in America, if you could have come to know just one man who wasn't restricted to boozing and womanizing. Perhaps you still can be."[5]

The two novelists met briefly in 1940 in Key West. Hemingway was then married to Martha Gellhorn, and Lewis was travelling with Marcella Powers. Lewis wrote in 1942 that Hemingway was "a jolly and amiable fellow to meet, yet he is also a lone scarred tree, for the lightning of living has hit him."[6] Lewis went on to say that *For Whom the Bell Tolls* was "a great love story, and a great *story,* . . . a dramatization of the revolution that is now altering the whole world." More interesting is Lewis's understanding of Hemingway's efforts to clear away quixotism: "Robert Jordan is a fighter, trained and formidable, but he indicates how the world is changing by his freedom from all the phony heroics of Kipling and Richard Harding Davis." Kipling and Davis were, of course, heroes of Lewis's youth, and Lewis was their follower in his apprentice poetry and fiction. Lewis then added that Hemingway proves "that we are living in the first age of history that is really romantic and interesting, so that we need no gilt and costuming to trick it out."

Lewis and Hemingway met again in 1949. Hemingway was married to Mary Welsh, and Lewis's companion was Marcella's mother, Mrs. Powers. Mark Schorer writes that Mrs. Powers remembers Lewis's saying to Mrs. Hemingway that her marriage would last but one year.[7] Hemingway's response to Lewis's remark, to his work, to his successes (and probably to Lewis's violation of the Hemingway code by travelling with his mistress' mother) is the portrait of an unidentified writer (usually taken to be Lewis) in *Across the River and into the Trees.* The writer sits in a Venetian café all day and writes in his room all night, though his best work is far behind him. There is a vicious picture of the man: "He had a strange face like an over-enlarged, disappointed weasel or ferret," pock-marked and blemished "as the mountains of the moon seen through a cheap telescope." Colonel Cantwell asks, "Do you think that pock-marked jerk is really a writer?" He explains to Renata that a jerk "means a man who has never worked at his trade (*oficio*) truly. . . . "[8] There was indeed a difference in sensibility between the two writers, though both could assume the grand gesture. The difference, as we have noted, can be symbolized in society's expulsion of the quixotic Robert Cohn, and the reverse in Lewis: the dismissal of society by a likewise quixotic Arrowsmith, who has his author's approval in doing so.

Thomas Wolfe, on the other hand, created a quixotic figure in Eugene Gant and felt disposed to admire the hero of large and sentimental gestures. The relationship with Wolfe began with Lewis's praise in the Nobel speech: "There is Thomas Wolfe, a child of, I believe, thirty or younger, whose one and only novel, *Look Homeward, Angel,* is worthy to be compared with the best in our literary production, a Gargantuan creature with great gusto of life."[9] Wolfe was overcome by these words and by his subsequent meeting with Lewis. He responded with a portrait of Lewis in *You Can't Go Home Again.*[10] Lewis appears as "Lloyd McHarg," the chief figure in American letters. In the speech accepting the highest literary award, McHarg has praised the young protagonist-writer George Webber and George thinks it "one of the most generous acts he had ever known" (p. 538). George and McHarg meet in London. Wolfe describes McHarg's "feverishly nervous vitality, wire-taut tension, incessant activity" (p. 541). Introducing George to friends, McHarg delivers one of those imitations of after-dinner speakers for which Lewis himself was famous, ending, "How do you like that, George? . . . Does that get 'em? Is that the way they do it? Not bad, eh?" (p. 547). As he writes further about McHarg—begins dwelling on the meaning of McHarg—Wolfe bursts forth in great passion. In spite of success—because of it—McHarg knows "the disappointment of reaching for the flower and having it fade the moment your fingers touch it" (p. 560). This great literary honor having been attained, McHarg's moment was now over. But Wolfe understands the spirit of the quixote—of the artist's "invincible and unlearning youth, . . . the spirit of indomitable hope and unwavering adventure, the spirit that is defeated and cast down ten thousand times but that is lost beyond redemption never" (pp. 560–61). So McHarg had toured Europe, searching and drinking, and had finally taken the "cure," about which Wolfe comments that it is the cure "really, for life-hunger, for life-thirst, for life-triumph, for life-defeat, life-disillusionment, life-loneliness, and life-boredom—cure for devotion to men and for disgust of them." He calls McHarg "this wounded lion, this raging cat of life, forever prowling," "a good and noble human being." "How much integrity and courage and honesty was contained in that tormented tenement of fury and lacerated hurts."

Lewis did not acknowledge the accuracy of Wolfe's treatment of him: "He caught my nervousness and restlessness—that's about all."[11] Yet beyond the nervousness and restlessness, unquestionably some of McHarg's passion was drawn from Lewis. For instance, the journalist Frazier Hunt reported standing with Lewis amid the poverty of Glasgow's slums, the foulest Hunt had seen anywhere in the world. With fists clenched to heaven and tears on his cheeks, Lewis cried out, "I can't stand it any more. I can't stand it!" and raved, "God damn the society that will permit such poverty! God damn the religions that stand for such a putrid system! God damn 'em all!"[12] And the literary historian Perry Miller, to whom Lewis had shouted "I love America. I love it, but I don't like it," summed up his impressions of Lewis by asking about the source of Lewis's love and hate: "Where did the love come from that could pour upon these things with a passion so concentrated that the only relief permitted it was to lash out against the very objects to which it was inescapably and irrevocably bound?"[13]

Perhaps Wolfe's portrait of Sinclair Lewis as Lloyd McHarg comes close to suggesting the answer. The intense construction of a writing career was the outlet of that nervous, sensitive, yearning, and disillusioned man who, if he at times felt that "man building" had more dignity than "man writing" or "man thinking," nevertheless gave himself over to literature with passion and generosity; whose moments of doubt about his vocation could be swept away by his exuberant response to an injustice, a perception of character, or a promising young talent. Meanwhile, he plunged, lonely and desperate, into hard work. "The builder . . . concentrates on his building"—though indeed, Lewis, builder of novels, never lost sight of the fame, money, salvation, and solace that lay as rewards for hard work. Work was the shield against loneliness, against doubt, against mockery. Best of all, his shelf of books was proof of accomplishment; hours at the writing desk were after all as valuable as hours in the laboratory or at the surgical table. His books were the platform from which he could chide the wastrels and the charlatans who eat up one's time and energy with their frivolous and selfish demands. Hard work remained the final virtue. So, in his last year, though dying, he could be found writing feverishly at *World So Wide*, fragments of other novels, and romantic poems again.

He had lived and written the story of the quixote, had taken arms to venture forth to conquer, had fought for reform, had achieved the goal of his quest by receiving the Nobel Prize for Literature, had defended his princesses, the weak, the oppressed. His quixotic adventure into life and craft became an education in reality. He set out eagerly, yet his exuberance was attended by considerable pain, and all along the way his quest was characterized by wavering, repetition, and difficulty in exploring fresh territory. For, curiously, even as he admired the "scientific era" (and the imperatives of realism), it may be that he was trying to preserve some of the romance "that must—or we die!—lie beyond the hills," as Hawk Ericson had exclaimed.

Lewis's use of quixotism brought to us a view of ourselves which we needed—and still need. Quixotes remain among the archetypes of American literature, along with the Adamic innocent and the Faustian rebel—from *Modern Chivalry* and *The Connecticut Yankee* to *The Adventures of Augie March, The Catcher in the Rye*, and Faulkner's trilogy. They are useful in portraying our fanciful vision of life, our chivalric impulses, our foolhardiness, our compulsion to aid the world and to fight its battles everywhere, our ambition to right all wrongs. We are befuddled into embarking on crusades; we undertake improbable wars; we are duped in our generous trade deals. Our idealism is admirable in motive, yet would benefit from reexamination. The national quixotism needs its cure. In his time Lewis made an effort to heal it (not always successfully, as we have seen). Lewis tried to undertake to do again "that good work done by Cervantes" (as Mark Twain put it) in purging the national culture of its foolishness once more.

Throughout this book on Lewis I have been attempting to deal with a writer, who, unlike any other major writer of his time, presents initial obstacles for the reader which are so spiky that one wonders how one is to surmount them to approach an evaluation of the enduring qualities of his work. There are, first, the books established on the mushy ground of such trivial notions as "play." There are the badly conceived books even after his apprentice days had ended—books like *Mantrap, Work of Art, Bethel Merriday, The God-Seeker, World So Wide.* In his best books there are many pages of poor prose and absurd notions. But I have tried to suggest that Lewis, born in a transitional age in American literary history and being a brash youth with few of the "standards" which in the Nobel speech he lamented were needed in American literature, had to fight his way through the appeal and the repulsion of cults and fads before he could establish a position from which, first, to direct his satire, and, second, to sustain his documentation of reality. If, now, at the end of this study, we have gained some understanding of the evolution of Lewis's imagination and have examined his skill in reporting some of the argument of American society and some of the concerns of American individuals, then we can ask, hasn't Lewis left us one additional gift? For it his idol, Dickens, served him well. The search for the value of American life continues—in society and within ourselves. In fact, it has intensified. His representation of it can move us by its terrible sense of pain and urgency. Furthermore, though the atmosphere of language in which his seekers wandered was noxious, by pushing his fantastic power of mimicry to the limit, he prophesied the crazier oratory of our day. The editorialist; the racist preacher; the retired militarist; the professorial hireling; the rationalist for defoliation; the ad-writer for half-empty boxes; the "poemulator" who sells millions of books and phonograph records; the leering sexologist; the inciter of violence; the astrology cultist; the talkers, talkers, talkers—they all pollute the air. But whether they know it or not, they squawk through loudspeakers and gesticulate before distortion mirrors that Sinclair Lewis set up a generation ago.

Notes

Preface

1. Mark Schorer, *Sinclair Lewis: An American Life* (New York: McGraw-Hill, 1961), and Sheldon Grebstein, *Sinclair Lewis,* United States Authors Series (New York: Twayne, 1962).

2. " 'Don Quixote' and 'Moby Dick' " in *Cervantes Across the Centuries,* eds. Angel Flores and M. J. Benardete (New York: Gordian Press, 1969), p. 227.

3. Joseph Harkey, "Don Quixote and American Fiction Through Mark Twain." (Ph.D. diss., University of Tennessee, 1967); Harry Levin, "The Quixotic Principle" in *The Interpretation of Narrative: Theory and Practice,* Harvard English Studies, 1, ed. Morton W. Bloomfield (Cambridge: Harvard University Press, 1970); Ihab Hassan, *Radical Innocence: The Contemporary American Novel* (Princeton: Princeton University Press, 1961); Theodore Gross, *The Heroic Ideal in American Literature* (New York: Free Press, 1971).

4. *Mississippi,* Stormfield Edn. (New York: Harper, 1929), pp. 337–78.

5. James Lundquist develops this idea in *Sinclair Lewis* (New York: Frederick Ungar, 1973), esp. pp. 18–19.

Chapter 1

1. "This Golden Half-Century, 1885–1935," *Good Housekeeping* 100 (May 1935); *MFMS,* p. 254 (see the Preface for the complete bibliographical entry for this book and other useful works abbreviated below).

2. "That Was New York and That Was Me," *New Yorker,* 2 January 1937, pp. 20–21; in *MFMS* from an original MS under the title "My First Day in New York," pp. 57–58.

3. "Introduction," *Cervantes: A Collection of Critical Essays,* Twentieth Century Views (Englewood Cliffs, N.J.: Prentice-Hall, Inc., 1969), p. 11.

4. *The Sun Also Rises* (New York: Scribner's, 1926), p. 9.

5. From *John Bull's Other Island and Major Barbara* (New York, 1908), p. 158 (Preface to *Major Barbara*) and *Les Faux-monnayeurs* (Paris, 1925), p. 261 in Levin, "The Quixotic Principle," Morton W. Bloomfield, ed. *The Interpretation of Narrative: Theory and Practice,* Harvard English Studies, 1 (Cambridge: Harvard University Press, 1970), p. 58.

6. Levin, "Principle," p. 65.

7. Ibid., p. 50.

8. Richard Predmore, *The World of Don Quixote* (Cambridge: Harvard University Press, 1967), p. 53.

9. *SL: Life,* passim.

10. "The Earlier Lewis," *Saturday Review,* 20 January 1934, p. 421.

11. L to H, 30 June 1919, *FMSTS,* pp. 7–8.

12. Constance Rourke, *American Humor: A Study of the National Character*

(New York: Doubleday, 1953), p. 222; Mark Schorer, "Sinclair Lewis: *Babbitt*" in Hennig Cohen, ed. *Landmarks of American Writing* (New York: Basic Books, 1969), p. 327.

13. See Carl L. Anderson, *The Swedish Acceptance of American Literature* (Philadelphia: University of Pennsylvania Press, 1957), p. 7.

14. Letters quoted in Carl Van Doren, *Three Worlds* (New York: Harper, 1936), pp. 146, 153–59; *MFMS*, pp. 135, 139–41.

15. L to H, 28 December 1920, *FMSTS*, p. 59; L to H and B, 5 November 1921, *FMSTS*, p. 87.

16. "Introduction," *Selected Short Stories*, p. x; *MFMS*, p. 219.

17. "Self-Portrait (Berlin, August, 1927)," *MFMS*, p. 48.

18. Allen Austin, "An Interview with Sinclair Lewis," *University Review* 24 (March 1958): 204.

19. Ibid., p. 201.

20. "Breaking into Print," *The Colophon*, no. 2, New Series (Winter 1937): 218; *MFMS*, p. 74.

21. "Rambling Thoughts on Literature as a Business," *Yale Literary Magazine* 100 (1936); *MFMS*, p. 197.

22. "The Death of Arrowsmith," *Coronet* 10 (July 1941): 108; *MFMS*, pp. 106–107.

23. "Unknown Undergraduates," *Yale Literary Magazine* 71 (June 1906): 335; *MFMS*, p. 122.

24. "Self-Portrait (Berlin)," *MFMS*, p. 46. When he wrote this essay, Lewis had yet to conceive of other admirable characters such as Dodsworth, Edith Cortright, Doremus Jessup, and Cass Timberlane.

25. Ibid, p. 48.

26. Ibid, p. 47.

27. "Sinclair Lewis," in *Spokesmen* (New York: Appleton, 1928), p. 219.

Chapter 2

1. "Self-Portrait (Berlin)," *MFMS*, p. 51.

2. "Self-Portrait (Nobel Foundation), 1930," *MFMS*, p. 55.

3. "A Minnesota Diary," ed. Mark Schorer, *Esquire* 50 (October 1958): 161.

4. *The Ferment of Realism: American Literature 1884–1919* (New York: Free Press, 1965), p. 1.

5. Ibid, p. 9.

6. *Homage to Theodore Dreiser* (New York: Random House, 1971), p. 63.

7. *American Writing in the Twentieth Century* (Cambridge: Harvard University Press, 1960), p. 1.

8. Ibid, p. 2.

9. "Defenders of Ideality," *Literary History of the United States*, rev. edn., ed. Robert E. Spiller, et. al. (New York: Macmillan, 1963), p. 813.

10. *The Poems of Thomas Bailey Aldrich* (Boston: Houghton Mifflin, 1893), pp. 17–18.

11. *Songs from Vagabondia* (Boston: Copeland and Day, 1894), p. 1.

12. *Ferment of Realism*, pp. 30–31.

13. *Intellectual Vagabondage: An Apology for the Intelligentsia* (New York: Doran, 1926).
14. *SL: Life*, pp. 123–25.
15. These poems and the story are from the *Yale Courant:* "When Viziers Speak," 24 December 1904; "A Summer's Tale," 8 April 1905; "A May Time Carol," 18 June 1904; "The Royal Glamour," 10 December 1904.
16. *The Americans 1890s: Life and Times of a Lost Generation* (New York: Viking, 1966), p. 78.
17. "The American Fear of Literature: The Nobel Prize Address, 1930," *MFMS*, pp. 15–16.
18. "Elsewhere" and this essay rpt. *MFMS*, pp. 114–15; 119–22.
19. "The Incorruptible Sinclair Lewis," *Atlantic* 187 (April 1951): 30–34.
20. *John Dos Passos' "Manhattan Transfer"* (New York: Harper, 1926), pp. 7–8; a shorter version of this booklet appeared in *Saturday Review*, 5 December 1925, p. 361.
21. "A Generation Nourished on H. G. Wells," *New York Herald Tribune Book Review*, 20 October 1946; rpt. as "Our Friend, H.G." in *MFMS*, pp. 246–53. Quotation in *MFMS*, p. 253.
22. "Foreword" to H. G. Wells, *The History of Mr. Polly* (New York: Readers Club, 1941), p. v.
23. "Our Friend, H. G.," *MFMS*, p. 253.
24. I have reprinted the exchange of letters between Lewis and Wells and have dealt fully with their relationship in "H. G. Wells and Sinclair Lewis: Friendship, Literary Influence, and Letters," *English Literature in Transition (1880–1920)* 5 (1962): 1–20.
25. "Foreword," p. vii.
26. The relationship is studied in Arthur B. Coleman, "The Genesis of Social Ideas in Sinclair Lewis," (Ph.D. diss., New York University, 1954).
27. "I'm an Old Newspaperman Myself," *Cosmopolitan* 122 (April 1947): 155–56; *MFMS*, p. 89.
28. Quoted in Alfred Kazin, *On Native Grounds* (New York: Reynal and Hitchcock, 1942), p. 98.
29. "American Fear"; *MFMS*, p. 8.
30. *Spokesmen*, (New York: Appleton, 1928), pp. 225–26.
31. "Four American Impressions," *New Republic*, 11 Oct. 1922, p. 172.
32. "Obscenity and Obscurity," *Esquire* 24 (July 1945): 51; *MFMS*, p. 208–209.
33. *The Twenties* (New York: Viking, 1955).
34. L to H, 30 October 1920, *FMSTS*, p. 40.
35. "The Library," *American Mercury* 10 (April 1927): 506.
36. "American Fear," *MFMS*, pp. 4–17.
37. *Letters of H. L. Mencken*, ed. Guy J. Forgue (New York: Knopf, 1961), p. 491.

Chapter 3

1. "The American Scene in Fiction," *New York Herald Tribune Book Review*, 14 April 1929; *MFMS*, p. 142.

2. Ibid.
3. "The Long Arm of the Small Town," *MFMS,* pp. 271–72.
4. "Minnesota, The Norse State," *Nation,* 30 May 1923, p. 627; *MFMS,* p. 283.
5. Quotations that follow from "Norse State," pp. 624–27; *MFMS,* pp. 273–83.
6. "Introduction," *Main Street* (New York: Limited Editions Club, 1937); pp. viii–ix; *MFMS,* p. 214.
7. See the Preface for a list of Lewis's books and for a statement about references to them.
8. *Civilization in the United States* (New York: Harcourt, 1922).
9. "The American Fear of Literature," *MFMS,* p. 7.
10. "Unpublished Introduction to Babbitt," part of a notebook in the Lewis Collection at Yale Library; *MFMS,* pp. 24, 29, 27.
11. "Back to Vermont," *The Forum,* 95 (April 1936): 254; *MFMS,* p. 284.
12. "A Minnesota Diary," ed. Mark Schorer, *Esquire* 50 (October 1958): 162.
13. "Self-Portrait (Nobel Foundation)," *MFMS,* p. 55.

Chapter 4

1. "I'm an Old Newspaperman Myself," *Cosmopolitan* 122 (April 1947): pt. 2; *MFMS,* p. 93.
2. *SL: Life,* p. 192.
3. New York: Readers Club, 1942, p. iii.
4. *Gracie,* p. 9.
5. Ibid., pp. 152–53.
6. Ibid., p. 306.
7. George Gordon [Charles C. Baldwin], *The Men Who Make Our Novels* (New York: Moffatt, Yard, 1919), pp. 225–26.
8. "Self-Portrait (Berlin, August 1927)," *MFMS,* p. 49.
9. "The Long Arm of the Small Town," *The O-Sa-Ge* (Sauk Centre, Minn., 1931), p. 83; *MFMS,* p. 272.
10. "Breaking into Print," *The Colophon,* no. 2, New Series (Winter 1937): 218; *MFMS,* p. 71.
11. "Sinclair Lewis vs. His Education," *Saturday Evening Post,* 26 December 1931, p. 20.
12. "Old Newspaperman," in *MFMS,* p. 79 (this section of the essay does not appear in the original version).
13. Ibid., p. 78.
14. "The Example of Cervantes," in Lowry Nelson, Jr., *Cervantes: A Collection of Critical Essays* (Englewood Cliffs, N.J.: Prentice-Hall, Inc. 1969), p. 36.
15. "Sinclair Lewis," *American Mercury* 53 (October 1941): 454.
16. *Gracie,* pp. 88–89.
17. Ibid., p. 90.
18. "Lewis vs. His Education," p. 21.
19. According to Harrison Smith, Lewis remembered being "drafted to assist in surgical operations by giving the anesthetic or sterilizing implements." Oliver Harrison, pseud., *Sinclair Lewis* (New York: Harcourt, 1925), pp. 3–4.

20. *Ann Vickers,* p. 16.
21. *Cass Timberlane,* pp. 52–53.
22. "A Village Radical: His Last American Home," *Venture* 2 (Winter 1957): 45.
23. See Montgomery Belgion, "How Sinclair Lewis Works," *The Bookman* (of London) 65 (January 1924): 195–96.
24. Perry Miller, "The Incorruptible Sinclair Lewis," *Atlantic* 187 (April 1951): 32.

Chapter 5

1. *Wrenn,* p. 16. See also *Cass Timberlane* in 1945: the judge spends lonely hours talking to a cat.
2. "Breaking into Print" *The Colophon,* no. 2, New Series (Winter 1937); *MFMS,* p. 73.
3. *Gracie,* pp. 70–71.
4. L to H, 30 November 1920, *FMSTS,* p. 52.
5. Letter of October 1921 in Van Doren, *Three Worlds* (New York:Harper, 1936), pp. 155–56; *MFMS,* p. 138.
6. *Saturday Evening Post,* 14 October 1916, p. 28.
7. *Good Housekeeping* 65 (September 1917), 25–28.
8. *Century Magazine* 94 (June 1917), 188–98.
9. *Gracie,* p. 109.
10. *Free Air* (New York: Harcourt, 1919) was preceded by *The Innocents: A Story for Lovers* (New York: Harper, 1917), an elderly couple's adventure across America. It was dedicated to Wells, among others, and to people who love Dickens. Lewis reluctantly acknowledged some doubts about this book himself; to Harcourt he wrote in mid-May 1920: "Don't you think it would be much better to *leave out The Innocents*—not take it over at all, or if you have to take it with the rest, not republish it? The general opinion seems to be very strongly that it is too sentimental to be in agreement with the other books, and republishing it might do more harm than good"; *FMSTS,* p. 28.

Chapter 6

1. L to H, 15 December 1919, *FMSTS,* p. 19.
2. L to H, 24 December 1919, *FMSTS,* p. 21.
3. L to H, 8 February 1920, *FMSTS,* p. 25.
4. L to H, 8 May 1920, *FMSTS,* p. 27.
5. "Introduction" to *Main Street* (Limited Editions Club), p. xi; *MFMS,* p. 216.
6. "Breaking into Print," *The Colophon,* no. 2, New Series (Winter 1937); *MFMS,* p. 74.
7. Betty Stevens, "A Village Radical: His Last American Home," *Venture* 2 (Winter 1957):37.
8. Perry Miller, "The Incorruptible Sinclair Lewis," *Atlantic* 187 (April 1951): 34.
9. "Introduction" to *Main Street; MFMS,* p. 215.

10. *The Gates of Horn: A Study of Five French Realists* (New York: Oxford University Press, 1963), p. 255.

11. In a fine essay on the dissociation of Lewis's characters from American society, Howell Daniels calls attention to the way in which Carol Kennicott, like Isabel Archer, exemplifies "what T. S. Eliot has called *bovarysme,* the adoption of an aesthetic rather than a moral attitude towards life," her romantic imagination deriving from fiction and poetry and from the "grandeur of the prairie." "Sinclair Lewis and the Drama of Dissociation," Malcolm Bradbury and David Palmer, eds. *The American Novel and the Nineteen Twenties,* Stratford-upon-Avon Studies, 13 (London: Edward Arnold, 1971), p. 91. Some early reviewers had seen *Main Street* as an American *Madame Bovary,* but only in brief comparisons; see Stuart Sherman, "The Significance of Sinclair Lewis," *Points of View* (New York: Scribner's, 1924), pp. 204–209.

12. *Gates of Horn,* p. 257.

13. *SL: Life,* p. 102.

14. "The Quixotic Principle," Morton W. Bloomfield, ed. *The Interpretation of Narrative: Theory and Practice,* Harvard English Studies, 1 (Cambridge: Harvard University Press, 1970), p. 65.

15. *Nation,* 10 September 1924, pp. 255–60; *MFMS,* pp. 310–27.

Chapter 7

1. "The American Scene in Fiction"; *MFMS,* p. 145.
2. L to H, 30 November 1920, *FMSTS,* p. 52.
3. L to H, 28 December 1920, *FMSTS,* p. 59.
4. L to H, 12 February 1922, *FMSTS,* p. 97.
5. L to H and B, 5 November 1921, *FMSTS,* p. 87.
6. Thus Frederick J. Hoffman sees two Babbitts in the novel: the parody Babbitt is one character, "a perfect representation of its limited kind"; the other is sensitive and humane, but "cancels the validity and nullifies the success" of the first. *The Twenties* (New York: Viking, 1949), p. 369.
7. L to H, 28 December 1920, *FMSTS,* p. 59.
8. Sheldon Grebstein, *Sinclair Lewis,* United States Authors Series (New York: Twayne, 1962) pp. 84–85.
9. Howell Daniels, "Sinclair Lewis and the Drama of Dissociation." Malcolm Bradbury and David Palmer, eds. *The American Novel and the Nineteen Twenties,* Stratford-upon-Avon Studies, 13 (London: Edward Arnold, 1971), pp. 94–95.

Chapter 8

1. "How I Wrote a Novel on Trains and beside the Kitchen Sink," *The American Magazine* 41 (April 1921): 114; *MFMS,* p. 206.
2. L to H, 13 December 1921, *FMSTS,* p. 90.
3. L to H and B, undated (January 1923?), *FMSTS,* p. 122.
4. L to H and others, 13 February 1923, *FMSTS,* p. 125.
5. "Self-Portrait (Berlin)," *MFMS,* p. 46.

6. "Self-Portrait (Nobel Foundation)," *MFMS,* p. 52.
7. *How to Read a Novel* (New York: Viking, 1957), p. 171.
8. "Techniques of Fiction," *Sewanee Review* 52 (1944): 210–15.
9. *The American Novel,* rev. edn. (New York: Macmillan, 1940), p. 308.
10. "How Good Is Sinclair Lewis?" *College English* 39 (January 1948): 178.
11. *The Literary Fallacy* (Boston: Little, Brown, 1944), p. 100.
12. "Sinclair Lewis," *Saturday Review,* 28 January 1933, p. 398.
13. Hans Zinsser, *Rats, Lice and History* (Boston: Little, Brown, 1935), p. 13.
14. Carl Van Doren, *Three Worlds* (New York: Harper, 1936), p. 308; DeVoto, "Sinclair Lewis," *Saturday Review,* p. 398.
15. "Interpreter of American Life," *Dial* 78 (June 1925): 518.

Chapter 9

1. "Sinclair Lewis and the Method of Half-Truths," *Society and Self in the Novel: English Institute Essays,* ed. Mark Schorer (New York: Columbia University Press, 1956), pp. 127–31.
2. Sharon's resemblance to traits of Aimee Semple MacPherson seems obvious.
3. "Method of Half-Truths," p. 131.
4. D. J. Dooley, *The Art of Sinclair Lewis* (Lincoln: University of Nebraska Press, 1967), p. 128.
5. *On the Meaning of Life,* ed. Will Durant (New York: Long and Smith, 1932); *MFMS,* pp. 41–42.
6. "Sinclair Lewis Introduces Elmer Gantry," *The Strange Necessity* (London: Jonathan Cape, 1928), pp. 275–80.

Chapter 10

1. Lewis's attitude toward Jews has been written about by Robert F. Fleissner as "L'Affaire Sinclair Lewis: 'Anti-Semitism?' and Ancillary Matters," *Sinclair Lewis Newsletter* 4 (1972): 14–16. I would like to say more about this matter another time. For the moment, I think that what Irving Howe has said of Sherwood Anderson in this regard can apply to Lewis. Anderson's treatment of Jews, Howe says, indicates that in addition to tolerance "there remained in him a preconscious remnant of that folk stereotype which regards Jews as the archetypal 'other,' alien, unknowable, and perhaps suspect." *Sherwood Anderson* (New York: William Sloane, 1951), p. 188.
2. Sheldon Grebstein, *Sinclair Lewis,* United States Authors Series (New York: Twayne, 1962), p. 117.
3. "A Minnesota Diary," ed. Mark Schorer, *Esquire* 50 (October 1958): 162.

Chapter 11

1. See Sheldon Grebstein, "Sinclair Lewis and the Nobel Prize," *Western Humanities Review* 13 (Spring 1959): 163–71; Martin Light, "A Further Word on Sinclair Lewis's Prize-Consciousness," *WHR* 15 (Autumn 1961): 368–371; William J. Stuckey, *The Pulitzer Prize Novels: A Critical Backward Look* (Norman: University of Oklahoma Press, 1966), pp. 58–60.

2. L to Ellen Eayrs, 12 November 1919, *FMSTS*, p. 18.
3. L to H, 4 April 1926, *FMSTS*, p. 203.
4. L to H, 15 January 1921, *FMSTS*, p. 61.
5. L to H, 26 March 1925, *FMSTS*, p. 180.
6. H to L, 10 April 1925, *FMSTS*, p. 184.
7. "Self-Portrait (Nobel Foundation)," *MFMS*, p. 55.
8. "The American Fear of Literature," *MFMS*, pp. 5, 6, 7.
9. "Unknown Undergraduates"; *MFMS*, p. 122.
10. "Mr. Lorimer and Me," *Nation*, 25 July 1928, p. 81.
11. "A Note About Kingsblood Royal," *Wings, The Literary Guild Review* (June 1947): pp. 4–10; *MFMS*, pp. 37–41.
12. "Sinclair Lewis: A Portrait," *American Scholar* 23 (Spring 1954): 174.

Chapter 12

1. Betty Stevens, "A Village Radical: His Last American Home," *Venture* 2 (Winter 1957): 42.
2. "The American Fear of Literature," *MFMS*, pp. 16–17.
3. New York: Scribner's, 1935, p. 19.
4. "Literary Felonies," *Saturday Review*, 3 October 1936, p. 3.
5. "Glorious Dirt," *Newsweek*, 18 October 1937, p. 34.
6. "Introduction" to Ernest Hemingway, *For Whom the Bell Tolls* (New York: Limited Editions Club, 1942), pp. ix–xi.
7. *SL Life*, pp. 780–81.
8. New York: Scribner's, 1950, pp. 87, 97.
9. "American Fear," *MFMS*, p. 17.
10. New York: Harper, 1934, chapters 33–37.
11. Allen Austin, "An Interview with Sinclair Lewis," *University Review* 24 (March 1958): 208.
12. *One American* (New York: Simon and Schuster, 1938), pp. 252–53.
13. Perry Miller, "The Incorruptible Sinclair Lewis," *Atlantic* 187 (April 1951): 31.

Selected Bibliography

Works by Lewis:

A list of Lewis's novels will be found in the Preface to this book. Therein one can also find a list of books that contain selections from Lewis's essays, short stories, and letters. In addition there are:

Jayhawker. A play, in collaboration with Lloyd Lewis. Garden City: Doubleday, Doran, 1935.

It Can't Happen Here: A New Version. New York: Dramatists Play Service, 1938.

I'm a Stranger Here Myself and Other Stories. Selected with an Introduction by Mark Schorer. Dell Laurel Edition. New York: Dell, 1962.

Storm in the West. A screenplay, in collaboration with Dore Schary. New York: Stein and Day, 1963.

For a complete bibliography of Lewis's writings refer to "A Sinclair Lewis Checklist" in Schorer's biography, pp. 815–26 (see below).

Book-length studies of Lewis:

Dooley, D. J. *The Art of Sinclair Lewis.* Lincoln: University of Nebraska Press, 1967.

Grebstein, Sheldon N. *Sinclair Lewis.* United States Authors Series. New York: Twayne, 1962.

Lewis, Grace H. *With Love from Gracie: Sinclair Lewis, 1912–1925.* New York: Harcourt, Brace, 1955.

Lundquist, James. *Sinclair Lewis.* Modern Literature Monographs. New York: Frederick Ungar Publishing Co., 1973.

O'Connor, Richard. *Sinclair Lewis.* American Writers Series. New York: McGraw-Hill, 1971.

Schorer, Mark. *Sinclair Lewis: An American Life.* New York: McGraw-Hill, 1961.

Sheean, Vincent. *Dorothy and Red.* Boston: Houghton Mifflin, 1963.

Books:

Baden, A. L., ed. *To the Young Writer.* Ann Arbor: University of Michigan Press, 1965 [Mark Schorer, "The Burdens of Biography"].

Bloomfield, Morton W., ed. *The Interpretation of Narrative: Theory and Practice.* Harvard English Studies, 1. Cambridge: Harvard University Press, 1970 [Harry Levin, "The Quixotic Principle"].

Bode, Carl, ed. *The Young Rebel in American Literature.* London: Heinemann, 1959 [Geoffrey Moore, "Sinclair Lewis: A Lost Romantic"].

Bradbury, Malcolm and David Palmer, eds. *The American Novel and the Nineteen Twenties.* Stratford-upon-Avon Studies, 13. London: Edward Arnold, 1971 [Howell Daniels, "Sinclair Lewis and the Drama of Dissociation"].

Cohen, Hennig, ed. *Landmarks of American Writing.* New York: Basic Books, 1969 [Mark Schorer, "Sinclair Lewis: *Babbitt*"].

Cowley, Malcolm, ed. *After the Genteel Tradition.* New York: Norton, 1937 [Robert Cantwell, "Sinclair Lewis"].

DeVoto, Bernard. *The Literary Fallacy.* Boston: Little, Brown, 1944.

French, Warren G. and Kidd, Walter E., eds. *American Winners of the Nobel Literary Prize.* Norman: University of Oklahoma Press, 1968 [Robert J. Griffin, "Sinclair Lewis"].

Forster, E. M. *Abinger Harvest.* New York: Harcourt, Brace, 1936.

Gardiner, Harold C., ed. *Fifty Years of the American Novel.* New York: Scribner's, 1952 [C. Carroll Hollis, "Sinclair Lewis: Reviver of Character"].

Geismar, Maxwell. *American Moderns: From Rebellion to Conformity.* New York: Hill and Wang, 1958.

———. *The Last of the Provincials: The American Novel 1915–1925.* Boston: Houghton Mifflin, 1947.

Griffin, Robert J., ed. *Twentieth Century Interpretations of "Arrowsmith."* Englewood Cliffs, N. J.: Prentice-Hall, 1968.

Gross, Theodore. *The Heroic Ideal in American Literature.* New York: Free Press, 1971.

Hassan, Ihab. *Radical Innocence: The Contemporary American Novel.* Princeton: Princeton University Press, 1961.

Hemingway, Ernest. *Across the River and into the Trees.* New York: Scribner's, 1950.

Hilfer, Anthony Channell. *The Revolt from the Village.* Chapel Hill: University of North Carolina Press, 1969.

Hoffman, Frederick J. *The Twenties: American Writing in the Postwar Decade.* New York: Viking, 1955.

Hunt, Frazier. *One American and His Attempt at Education.* New York: Simon and Schuster, 1938.

Kazin, Alfred. *On Native Grounds: An Interpretation of Modern American Prose Literature.* New York: Reynal and Hitchcock, 1942.

Light, Martin, ed. *Studies in "Babbitt."* Columbus, Ohio: Charles E. Merrill, 1971.

Lundquist, James. *Guide to Sinclair Lewis.* Columbus, Ohio: Charles E. Merrill, 1970.

Madden, David, ed. *American Dreams and American Nightmares.* Carbondale: Southern Illinois University Press, 1970 [James C. Austin, "Sinclair Lewis and Western Humor"].

Millgate, Michael. *American Social Fiction, James to Cozzens.* Edinburgh: Oliver and Boyd, 1964.

Nelson, Lowry, Jr., ed. *Cervantes: A Collection of Critical Essays.* Twentieth Century Views. Englewood Cliffs, N. J.: Prentice-Hall, 1969.

Predmore, Richard. *The World of Don Quixote.* Cambridge: Harvard University Press, 1967.

Rourke, Constance. *American Humor.* New York: Harcourt, Brace, 1931.

Schorer, Mark. *Sinclair Lewis.* University of Minnesota Pamphlets on American Writers, no. 27. Minneapolis: University of Minnesota Press, 1963.

Schorer, Mark, ed. *Sinclair Lewis: A Collection of Critical Essays.* Twentieth Century Views. Englewood Cliffs, N. J.: Prentice-Hall, 1962.

_______. *Society and Self in the Novel.* English Institute Essays. New York: Columbia University Press, 1955 [Mark Schorer, "Sinclair Lewis and the Method of Half Truths"].

Stegner, Wallace, ed. *The American Novel.* New York: Basic Books, 1965 [Daniel Aaron, "Sinclair Lewis, *Main Street*"].

Thorp, Willard. *American Writing in the Twentieth Century.* Cambridge: Harvard University Press, 1960.

Tuttleton, James W. *The Novel of Manners in America.* Chapel Hill: University of North Carolina Press, 1972.

West, Rebecca. *The Strange Necessity.* New York: Doubleday, Doran, 1928.

Whipple, Thomas K. *Spokesmen.* New York: D. Appleton, 1928.

Wolfe, Thomas. *You Can't Go Home Again.* New York: Harper, 1934.

Periodical articles:

Aaron, Daniel. "Proud Prejudices of Sinclair Lewis." *Reporter* 9 (4 August 1953): 37–39.

Anderson, Sherwood. "Four American Impressions." *New Republic,* 11 October 1922, pp. 171–73.

Austin, Allen. "An Interview with Sinclair Lewis." *University Review* 24 (March 1958): 199–210.

Babcock, C. Merton. "Americanisms in the Novels of Sinclair Lewis." *American Speech* 35 (May 1960): 110–16.

Barry, James D. "*Dodsworth:* Sinclair Lewis's Novel of Character." *Ball State University Forum* 10 (Spring 1969): 8–14.

Beck, Warren. "How Good Is Sinclair Lewis?" *College English* 9 (January 1948): 173–80.

Benét, William Rose. "The Earlier Lewis." *Saturday Review,* 20 January 1934, pp. 421–22.

Brown, Daniel R. "Lewis's Satire—A Negative Emphasis." *Renascence* 18 (Winter 1966): 63–72.

Bucco, Martin. "The Serialized Novels of Sinclair Lewis." *Western American Literature* 4 (Spring 1969): 29–37.

Carpenter, Frederick I. "Sinclair Lewis and the Fortress of Reality." *College English* 16 (April 1955): 416–23.

Coard, Robert L. "Names in the Fiction of Sinclair Lewis." *Georgia Review* 16 (Fall 1962): 318–29.

Conroy, Stephen S. "Sinclair Lewis's Sociological Imagination." *American Literature* 42 (November 1970): 348–62.

Couch, William, Jr. "Sinclair Lewis: Crisis in the American Dream." *CLA Journal* 7 (March 1964): 224–34.

Douglas, George H. "*Main Street* After Fifty Years." *Prairie Schooner* 44 (Winter 1970/71): 338–48.

Fife, Jim L. "Two Views of the American West." *Western American Literature* 1 (1966): 34–43.

Flanagan, John T. "A Long Way to Gopher Prairie: Sinclair Lewis's Apprenticeship." *Southwest Review* 32 (Autumn 1947): 403–13.

———. "The Minnesota Backgrounds of Sinclair Lewis' Fiction." *Minnesota History* 37 (March 1960): 1–13.

Fleissner, Robert F. "L'Affaire Sinclair Lewis: 'Anti-Semitism?' and Ancillary Matters." *Sinclair Lewis Newsletter* 4 (1972): 14–16.

———. " 'Something out of Dickens' in Sinclair Lewis." *Bulletin of the New York Public Library* 74 (November 1970): 607–16.

Friedman, Philip Allan. "*Babbitt:* Satiric Realism in Form and Content." *Satire Newsletter* 4 (Fall 1966): 20–29.

Fyvel, T. R. "Martin Arrowsmith and His Habitat." *New Republic,* 18 July 1955, pp. 16–18.

Gauss, Christian. "Sinclair Lewis vs. His Education." *Saturday Evening Post,* 26 December 1931, pp. 19–21, 54–56.

Grebstein, Sheldon. "The Education of a Rebel: Sinclair Lewis at Yale." *New England Quarterly* 28 (September 1955): 372–82.

———. "Sinclair Lewis and the Nobel Prize." *Western Humanities Review* 13 (Spring 1959): 163–71.

———. "Sinclair Lewis' Minnesota Boyhood." *Minnesota History* 34 (Autumn 1954): 85–89.

———. "Sinclair Lewis's Unwritten Novel." *Philological Quarterly* 37 (October 1958): 400–409.

Gurko, Leo and Miriam. "The Two Main Streets of Sinclair Lewis." *College English* 4 (February 1943): 288–92.

Helleberg, Marilyn M. "The Paper-Doll Characters of Sinclair Lewis' *Arrowsmith.*" *Mark Twain Journal* 14 (1969): 17–21.

Howe, Irving, "The World He Mimicked Was His Own." *New York Times Book Review,* 1 October 1961, pp. 1, 34.

Kazin, Alfred. "Poor Old Red." *Reporter* 25 (9 November 1961): 60–64.

Lewis, Robert W. "*Babbitt* and the Dream of Romance." *North Dakota Quarterly* 40 (1972): 7–14.

Light, Martin. "H. G. Wells and Sinclair Lewis: Friendship, Literary Influence, and Letters." *English Literature in Transition, 1880–1920* 5 (1962): 1–20.

———. "Lewis' Finicky Girls and Faithful Workers." *University Review* 30 (Winter 1963): 151–59.

Manfred, Frederick F. "Sinclair Lewis: A Portrait." *American Scholar* 23 (Spring 1954): 162–84.

Miller, Perry. "The Incorruptible Sinclair Lewis." *Atlantic* 187 (April 1951): 30–34.

Petrullo, Helen B. "*Babbitt* as Situational Satire." *Kansas Quarterly* 1 (1969): 89–97.

———. "*Main Street, Cass Timberlane* and Determinism." *South Dakota Review* 7 (Winter 1969–70): 30–42.

Quivey, James R. "George Babbitt's Quest for Masculinity." *Ball State University Forum* 10 (1969): 4–7.

Rosenberg, Charles E. "Martin Arrowsmith: The Scientist as Hero." *American Quarterly* 15 (Fall 1963): 447–58.

Schorer, Mark. "The Monstrous Self-Deception of Elmer Gantry." *New Republic,* 31 October 1955, pp. 13–15.

———. "Two Houses, Two Ways: The Florentine Villas of Lewis and Lawrence Respectively." *New World Writing,* 4th Mentor Selection. New York: New American Library, 1953, pp. 136–54.

———. "The World of Sinclair Lewis." *New Republic,* 6 April 1953, pp. 18–20.

Schorer, Mark, ed. "A Minnesota Diary," *Esquire* 50 (October 1958): 160–62.

Sinclair Lewis Newsletter. St. Cloud, Minn.: St. Cloud State College, 1969– .

Spitz, Leon. "Sinclair Lewis' Prof. Gottlieb." *American Hebrew* 158 (3 December 1948): 2, 10.

Stevens, Betty. "A Village Radical Goes Home." *Venture* 2 (Summer 1956): 17–26.

———. "A Village Radical: His Last American Home." *Venture* 2 (Winter 1957): 35–48.

Stolberg, Benjamin. "Sinclair Lewis." *American Mercury* 53 (October 1941): 450–60.

Thompson, Dorothy. "The Boy and Man from Sauk Centre." *Atlantic* 206 (November 1960): 39–48.

———. "Sinclair Lewis: A Postscript." *Atlantic* 187 (June 1951): 73–74.

(For further bibliographical entries see James Lundquist, *Checklist of Sinclair Lewis.* Columbus, Ohio: Charles E. Merrill, 1970.)

Index